BUILDING PROJECT MANAGEMENT

CENTERS OF EXCELLENCE

✛

BUILDING PROJECT MANAGEMENT

CENTERS OF EXCELLENCE

✛

Dennis Bolles, PMP®

AMACOM
American Management Association
New York • Atlanta • Brussels • Buenos Aires • Chicago • London • Mexico City
San Francisco • Shanghai • Tokyo • Toronto • Washington, D.C.

Special discounts on bulk quantities of AMACOM books are available to corporations, professional associations, and other organizations. For details, contact Special Sales Department, AMACOM, a division of American Management Association, 1601 Broadway, New York, NY 10019.
Tel.: 212-903-8316. Fax: 212-903-8083.
Web site: www.amacombooks.org

"PMI" and the PMI logo are service and trademarks registered in the United States and other nations; "PMP" and the PMP logo are certification marks registered in the United States and other nations; "PMBOK," "PM Network," and "PMI Today" are trademarks registered in the United States and other nations; and "Project Management Journal" and "Building professionalism in project management." are trademarks of the Project Management Institute, Inc.

Library of Congress Cataloging-in-Publication Data

Bolles, Dennis.
    Building project management centers of excellence / by Dennis Bolles.
        p. cm.
Includes bibliographical references and index.
    ISBN 0-8144-0717-X
    1. Project management. I. Title.
    HD69.P75 B65 2002
    658.4'04—dc21

                                                  2002005265

Printing number

10 9 8 7 6 5 4 3 2 1

To my wife, Mary, who has
been encouraging and supportive
for the past 36 years, in spite of the anxiety
my many career changes have caused her.

CONTENTS

Preface. . . . .   *xi*

Acknowledgments. . . . .   *xiii*

SECTION I   Establishing the PMCoE   1

CHAPTER 1   Introduction   3

The Driving Forces   4

Giving It a Name   7

The Importance of Positioning   10

Project Management Must Be Viewed as a

    Business Function   11

Organization Structure   12

PMCoE Organization Roles   14

Summary   14

CHAPTER 2   Initiating the PMCoE Project.   19

Assess Knowledge and Skill Levels   19

Writing a Charter   21

Writing a Scope Statement   22

Assembling Project and Steering Teams   24

Hold a Kick-off Event.   25

Create Task Force Teams.   28

Four Key PMCoE Elements   29

Summary   32

CHAPTER 3   Creating and Managing A

Project Portfolio.   35

Identifying Organizational Goals and Objectives. . . .   35

Achieving Corporate Goals and Objectives 36
Hosin Kanri 38
Establish Project Portfolios 42
Capacity and Capability 43
The Project Portfolio and Capital Budget Plan 47
New Opportunities 48
Managing the Project Portfolio 48
PMCoE Logo 55
Summary 56

CHAPTER 4   Key Ingredients of a Methodology . . 57
Key Ingredients 58
Generic Methodology 59
Creating Classifications 61
Minimum Requirements for Early Implementers 62
Distributing a Project Management Methodology . . . 69
Summary 71

CHAPTER 5   Education and Training;
Critical Success Factors 73
The Importance of Education and Training 74
Elements of an Education and Training Program 74
The Internal Project Management
    Certification Program 77
Developing the Education and Training Program . . . 78
Summary 79

CHAPTER 6   Ready-Set-Go! 81
Performing a Readiness Review 82
Post Project Reviews 84
Summary 85

CHAPTER 7   Maturity Takes Time 87
Stages of Maturity 93
Benchmarking 96
Summary 99

SECTION II
Project Management Methodology Guidelines 101
CHAPTER 8   Introduction to a Methodology 103
Vision 103
Purpose 103

Implementation. 104
Methodology Overview 104
Core Process Integration. 105
Project Phase Definitions 106
Project Levels 106
CHAPTER 9 Project Authorization. 115
Section Overview 115
Project Request. 115
Project Charter 116
CHAPTER 10 Project Initiation. 119
Section Overview 119
Project Initiation Process. 119
CHAPTER 11 Project Planning. 123
Section Overview 123
Project Planning Process. 123
CHAPTER 12 Project Execution 127
Section Overview 127
Project Progress Reporting Cycle Process. 127
Project Issues Resolution Process 128
Project Change Control Process 131
CHAPTER 13 Project Closing. 139
Section Overview 139
Post Project Review Process 139
Metrics Reporting Process 140
CHAPTER 14 Education and Training 147
Section Overview 147
Education and Training Goals 147
Education and Training Requirements 147
Education and Training Curriculum. 150

Appendix A. 169

Appendix B. 189

Index. 235

PREFACE

In my book, *Winning in Business with Enterprise Project Management* (Amacom, NY, 1998), I gave the tongue-in-cheek title "Oh Give Me a Home" to the chapter about project offices. Here's why I used that title. In my consulting and training experiences, I have observed that most organizations do not have a common reference point for project methodologies, tools, and training. They also lack an "ambassador-ship" or spot for generating advocacy on the topic, similar to practices generally used for Total Quality programs popular in the 1980s.

Building Project Management Centers of Excellence presents a compelling argument for establishing such a "home" for project management at the highest levels within an organization. Dennis Bolles argues that this positioning is critical to the successful adoption of project management as an enterprise-wide business solution for achieving world-class status.

The author also points out that project offices may be found at different organizational levels and under varied names, including: CPMO (Corporate Project/Program Management Office), PMCoE (Project Management Center of Excellence), PMO (Project Management Office), PSO (Project Support Office), and PO (Project Office). The book focuses primarily on the PMCoE, based on the argument that it is primarily strategic in concept and is largely coincidental with the high-level CPMO view. The PMCoE's focus is Strategic Forecast Planning and the establishment of corporate standards that include the use of common management methodologies, processes, tools, templates, education, training, and project management competency.

Dennis Bolles supports the concept that project management should permeate the whole organization, thus justifying the need to have a PMCoE at a high level to ensure that project policies receive enough prestige and visibility to be put into practice. This means that across-the-board buy-in is required for all types of projects, from classic capital project undertakings and IT ventures, to marketing, continuous improvement, annual operational targets, and organizational change. A well-positioned PMCoE can be the key to ensuring that all types of projects are carried out effectively, no matter what their nature may be.

Building Project Management Centers of Excellent is a significant contribution to the growing field of literature on how to best foster excellence in project management in organizations. Dennis Bolles's substantial professional background qualifies him to put forth his experiences and views on the subject. He adds a rich collection of samples, tables, templates, and figures that illustrate how to pursue excellence in project management through the implementation of a PMCoE. I am pleased to recommend this book for those project professionals and executives who want to improve the quality of projects in their organizations.

Paul C. Dinsmore, PMP® and Fellow of PMI®
President, Dinsmore Associates
www.daconsult.com.br
e-mail: dinsmore@amcham.com.br

ACKNOWLEDGMENTS

I don't believe there are many people who have traveled life's pathways and enjoyed their careers as much as I have over the past 32 years. I attribute my satisfaction to three conditions that have significantly influenced my life: my early recognition of the creative and organizational talents that God blessed me with at birth; a loving wife and family who supported my many career changes; and many talented, skilled, and veteran professionals who have shared their knowledge and skills with me as we worked side by side. I am undeniably indebted.

Many of the ideas, concepts, and materials I have used in the development of this book come from collaborations and discussions of concepts with individuals throughout my career, and in many cases just from being allowed by my superiors the time to think about and create new project management concepts and approaches for delivering services, tools, and techniques. These are the people who have either inspired me the most or had a significant impact in other ways on my professional career: Gordon M. Buitendorp, Hugh Broersma, Steve Broersma, Bruce Jipping, Randy Bassin, Phil Nunn, James Stroop, Rex Bakker, Tom Start, John DeMaria, Larry Spoolstra, Dave Theriaul, Denis Couture, Larry Lacombe, Erro Gibbs, Dalton Weekly, Steve Neuendorf, Peter Rogers, William F. Bundy, Ric Byham, Elizabeth Mallory, Jim Teer, Tim Oglesby, Brendan O'Reilly, Kelly Talsma, Dr. Harold Kerzner, and Paul Campbell Dinsmore.

I particularly appreciate the permissions granted me by the following individuals and organizations for the materials they have allowed me to reprint in this book: Dwane Baumgardner, Chairman and CEO, Donnelly Corporation; the Donnelly Corporation; Pet Babich, President, Total Quality Engineering, Inc.; John Goodpasture, President, Square Peg Consulting, Inc.; Tom Mochal, Tenstep Web Master.

SECTION I

✢

Establishing the PMCoE

CHAPTER 1

Introduction

Today's global market companies, regardless of industry and size, are looking to improve their systems and processes to become more competitive. One way they are attempting to do this is by establishing project management as a core competency throughout the organization. By setting up standardized procedures within the company, they hope to learn from past mistakes, make processes more efficient, and develop people's skills and talents to work more effectively. This book is written for those organizations that are considering taking, or that have already taken, this first step, but are having difficulty gaining the level of acceptance necessary to achieve complete success. The list of organizations attempting to integrate project management disciplines and best practices into the way they manage their businesses is expanding daily; however, those who have *succeeded* in doing so is significantly smaller. The answer for many of these companies is positioning. By positioning we mean that the group charged with the implementation of project management and best practices is positioned in the uppermost levels of the firm. It is critical that all levels of workers and managers see that the executive level of the firm supports it without hesitation, publicly, and completely. Without support from the top, it won't get off the ground. Typically, the group charged with the responsibility to get the system up and running is called a Project Management Center of Excellence (PMCoE). Positioning is a critical aspect of establishing project management as a company's enterprise-wide core competency. It must first be viewed and treated as a key business function throughout the organization. It is the first critical step toward successfully institutionalizing project management best practices as a core competency. The first step that is required to achieve the goal of establishing project management enterprise-wide is the creation of a PMCoE that has the authority and responsibility to get the job done.

This book provides examples that show how to implement project management disciplines and practices successfully. Establishing project management centers of excellence should not be viewed as a quick-fix solution, but rather as a long-term, foundation-building effort. It is not a trivial pursuit. Deciding to establish an effective PMCoE is the opening action. It requires significant changes in organizational structure and obliges people at all levels in the company to learn new concepts of managing by applying new methods to complete the work they do. Careful planning with the tenacity to stay on track and not lose sight of the end goal is essential.

In this book, we identify the structural changes required; how to effectively manage and distribute company resources; how to develop and distribute an effective project management methodology; how to identify education and training criteria, curriculum, and performance evaluation methods; how to ensure a project's readiness before work begins; and, finally, how to identify the growth levels the organization must progress through as it matures.

The Driving Forces

Competing globally, increasing market share, reducing costs, and improving profits—all in the pursuit of producing better products and services faster through the use of high technology solutions—are just a few of the reasons why most organizations seek better ways to improve time-to-market, cost-to-market, and quality-to-market. The effective use of project management techniques is a critical element for achieving improvements in these areas. Some firms even view project management as a key weapon in their arsenal to increase customer satisfaction and beat the competition. Dr. Harold Kerzner, Executive Director for Project Management at the International Institute for Learning, states the case well in this excerpt from the preface of his book, *In Search of Excellence in Project Management:**

> *Project management is no longer viewed as a system internal to the organization. It is now viewed as a competitive weapon that brings quality and value added to the customer.*

Kerzner identifies twenty-seven companies that are considered world-class organizations that excel at using project management as a strategic management tool and that have either achieved some degree of excellence or are headed in the right direction to achieve excellence in the future.

The organization as a whole must recognize and adopt new attitudes that embrace project management best practices as the normal way of working. This enables them to bring the full power of this new competitive weapon to bear in the battle of continued business growth and, in many cases, ultimate survival in today's highly competitive global market.

PMCoEs are created for many different reasons; however, they typically share an origin that involves some degree of pain, which brings about a need to take action to relieve or eliminate the pain.

Changes often occur as a result of pain, which is caused by some circumstance—either internal or external—that is outside the control of the organization. Figure 1–1 shows a simple example of how changes typically come about. These circumstances may motivate organizations to establish a PMCoE. Some examples include:

- Losing market share due to increasing global competition
- Poor cost vs. profit ratios resulting in falling or stagnant stock values
- Competition with faster time-to-market
- Changing economic conditions that force downsizing
- Effective use of fewer resources caused by downsizing

------

*Harold Kerzner, *In Search of Excellence in Project Management* (New York: John Wiley & Sons, Inc., 1998).

Figure 1–1. Steps Leading to Change

The PAIN caused by driving force(s) must be strong enough to establish a NEED for relief.	NEED is translated into a desire to take ACTION that will provide a solution to remove the pain.	The ACTION taken is often in the form of a quick fix that provides short-term relief rather than a long-term solution to eliminate the root cause of the pain.

- Implementing new technology to become more efficient
- Managing changes brought on by dynamic growth
- New executives who have seen it add value elsewhere

Understanding the motive behind the decision to create a PMCoE is very important, because if the motive is unclear or poorly communicated, then defining the purpose, goals, and objectives of the PMCoE becomes challenging.

The desire to set up a PMCoE can originate from any level of the organization, but frequently emerges from an area of the organization whose projects have the greatest impact on all sectors of the company. Information Technology (IT) is typically the functional area where PMCoE start out in most organizations, regardless of industry. This happens for several reasons.

- The rapid growth in technology and desktop use of business applications have generated a large number of projects that affect the whole organization.
- IT is most often where the greatest number of strategic, mission-critical projects affecting the whole organization occur.
- The Y2K issue brought the effectiveness of project management to the forefront for many IT executives.
- IT consumes a significant portion of the annual operating budget in most large organizations, thereby giving mission-critical projects high visibility.

- Reports from IT watchdog groups, such as Gartner and Standish, indicate a poor record of successes for IT projects in general.

Where the PMCoE is positioned in the organization's management structure has a significant impact on the overall success of establishing project management disciplines enterprise-wide. Positioning also affects the title you give this function or unit and how you define the role it plays in the organization.

Giving It a Name

Assigning a name to a function gives it significance and differentiates it from other functions within the organization. The names or titles typically given to this function include:

- Corporate Project/Program Management Office (CPMO)
- Project Management Center of Excellence (PMCoE)
- Project Management Office (PMO)
- Project Support Office (PSO)
- Project Office (PO)

These titles are often used interchangeably, and it is usually a matter of personal preference rather than application of any particular standard. A recent effort by various authors who have written about the Project Office provides some definition for these titles. Table 1–1 contains the definitions used in this book, which are also being used in a number of organizations.

Two key issues affect the assigning of titles: first, defining where the function will reside within the organization structure (the direct line of report), and second, what purpose it will serve in that position. This second issue is discussed in greater detail in Chapter 2. Titles often add significance to the roles, responsibility, accountability, and requisite authority (RRAA) of the position. Table 1–2 provides brief descriptions for each of the roles listed in Table 1–1.

Table 1–1.   Project Management Organization Titles

Title (Focus)
Definition of Responsibility

CPMO (Strategic)
The CPMO is accountable for enterprise-wide distribution of project
   management best practices. The CPMO is a corporate business function with
   the title and responsibility similar to traditional business functions such as
   Finance, Engineering, Marketing/Sales, Manufacturing, Information
   Technology, etc., which provide leadership and have "ownership" of their
   respective functional disciplines.
PMCoE (Strategic)
The PMCoE is an alternative title for the CPMO and is the one used in this
   book because the name implies its primary mission and can be applied when
   the function is not positioned at the corporate level but has the same
   responsibilities. Its primary focuses are strategic forecast planning and the
   establishment of corporate standards that include the effective use of a
   common project management methodology, processes, tools, templates,
   education, training, and project management competency.
PMO (Tactical)
The PMO is responsible for tactical master planning within major divisions,
   business units, regions, etc., overseeing the effective application of the project
   management standards established by the PMCoE within their respective
   sphere of responsibility.
PSO (Operational)
The PSO is responsible for operational master planning, which oversees the
   effective application of the project management standards established by the
   PMCoE in direct support of all projects within a functional department.
PO (Operational)
The PO is responsible for the direct support of a single, mission-critical project,
   which is typically large and complex, and whose success affects multiple
   areas of the company.

The project management organization structure shown in Figure 1–2 illustrates how the PMCoE might be implemented in a large
organization with multiple divisions or business units or geograph-
ical regional operations. The number of layers and the number of
project management units within each layer depends on the size of
the unit, the number of annual projects in the portfolio, and the complexity of the projects within the various levels of the organization.
For small to mid-sized organizations, the number of layers and func-

Table 1–2. RRAA Matrix

Roles	Responsibility	Accountability	Requisite Authority
CPMO or PMCoE	Provides corporate vision, mission, goals, and objectives—strategic master planning.	Reports directly to the CEO/President (highest level corporate officer).	Reviews and approves annual corporate master project portfolio and master project capital budget plan.
PMO One for each division/business unit/region (quantity depends on several variables)	Provides tactical master planning and resource management.	Division/business unit/region—reports directly to PMCoE and dotted line to to executive VP/director.	Establishes annual master project portfolio and project capital plan and authorizes adjustments. Oversees enterprise-wide projects, such as ERP systems implementation or business process re-engineering efforts.
PSO One or more (quantity of PSOs depends on several variables)	Provides operational master planning and project portfolio management.	Functional department—reports directly to PMO and dotted line to VP/manager.	Develops annual master project portfolio operational plan and capital authorization request plan.
PO One for each major mission-critical project	Provides project implementation—initiation, planning, execution, control, and closing.	Large strategic project—reports to project manager who reports directly to the PSO.	Plans, manages, controls, and reports project progress.

tional units may be adjusted to fit the amount of control required by the project activity at each level. The need to accommodate different management styles, work environments, and product life cycle issues means there is no one-size-fits-all organization structure. The main concern in developing a project management organization structure is establishing the functional ownership and leadership of

Figure 1–2.   Project Management Organization Reporting Structure

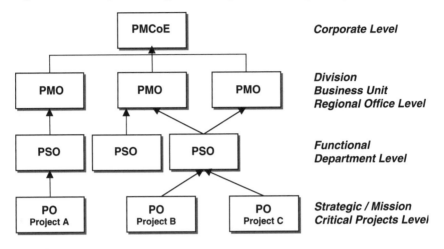

the discipline at the highest level within the company. Further decomposition of the project management structure depends on the amount of support and control required at each level.

As we mentioned earlier, titles also make a difference. Different titles eliminate confusion when communicating the distinctions among the various project management "offices" within the organization structure. It is important to note, however, that positioning the project management function in the organization's management structure has far more importance and has a greater impact on institutionalizing project management best practices than what title it is given.

Unfortunately, establishing a Project Office is most often done at a functional department level rather than at the corporate level. Positioning the office at the corporate level is especially important, however, if the long-term objective is to instill project management best practices in all areas of the company as a core competency.

The Importance of Positioning

Consider what would happen if a company did not have the typical business functional departments—engineering, finance, purchasing, etc.—established at the corporate level. Without these enterprise-wide business functions, the managers within each business unit would have to decide how engineering, finance, purchasing, etc., would be done in their areas of responsibility without considering the need to manage shared resources and communicate important information with other departments. Because the business functions critical to managing the company as a whole would differ from department to department, there would be few, if any, common processes. Work would be completed in an ad hoc environment, and chaos would be the rule of the day. Fortunately, most organizations understand the importance of establishing ownership and leadership of key business functions at the corporate level, and common processes and practices across the organization are the norm rather than the exception.

Positioning is equated with authority in organization structures; the closer something is to the top, the higher its level of autonomy, authority, and responsibility. Establishing project management in most organizations is very difficult to do, because managers are afraid of losing their authority and control over the resources that are assigned to them. Workers are afraid of being held accountable for performing a new set of requirements. This fear, expressed as resistance, comes from lack of information and understanding about how the changes will affect their jobs. Positioning the project management function at the highest level within the organization provides the measure of autonomy necessary to extend its authority across the organization while substantiating the value and importance the function has in the eyes of executive management.

Project Management as a Business Function

Project management has the greatest impact on a customer's recognition of an organization as a world-class leader in time-to-market, cost-to-market, and quality-to-market. Completing projects successfully on a consistent basis is a basic requirement to receive excellence awards from most customers. This is the goal of every organization. If projects are an integral part of the business, it stands to reason that there should be a clear understanding of what is and isn't a project, and what is required to satisfy the customer.

Organizations that sell products or services should recognize that their business livelihood depends on completing projects that directly affect their bottom line. They also should realize that completing projects successfully on a consistent basis requires the application of specific knowledge, skills, tools, and techniques. Doesn't it make sense then that such an important business function be established at the executive management level of the organization? How else can a company ensure that projects are managed successfully across the organization, and that strategic, mission-critical projects are given the best opportunity to succeed from the very start?

Organization Structure

Positioning the project management function in a hierarchical organization structure establishes its autonomy and thus "ownership" of the responsibility for setting up, distributing, supporting, and managing the application of project management best practices within the company, as shown in Figure 1–2.

Enterprise-wide adoption of project management best practices calls for single ownership of the function. Establishing common practices across an organization at all levels is very difficult, if not impossible, without a sole ownership being clearly established. Ownership must be recognized as an independent business function at the highest level of the organization to enable the authority that is required to distribute, monitor, and control the distribution of the disciplines required to achieve enterprise-wide project management best practice capabilities.

The next step is to determine how to begin putting the project management organization structure in place, starting with the PMCoE. Establishing the PMCoE organization structure is a significant undertaking. It will meet with resistance at various levels of the organization for many different reasons. One of the major reasons is the most obvious, but it is seldom given sufficient consideration. People generally resist changes because they don't understand why the changes are necessary and how the changes will impact them. Most prefer the status quo to doing something new, especially when it involves how they perform their work. Department managers, sometimes referred to as "the frozen middle," resist organizational changes because they fear they may lose their most valued employees—their project managers—if they are moved into a PMCoE/PMO/PSO as part of the restructuring process, and people = power in most companies.

Two typical scenarios describe where project managers could reside in a PMCoE organization structure, and hence where the shift in power will occur. Scenario 1 has all of the project managers reporting directly to the PMCoE with a dotted line responsibility to the function department where they previously resided. Scenario 2 is just the opposite, with the project managers remaining with and directly reporting to the functional department heads with a dotted line responsibility to the PMCoE as shown in Figure 1–3.

Table 1–3 lists some of the advantages and disadvantages of selecting scenario 1 over scenario 2.

The advantages noted in scenario 1 are certainly legitimate, however, they probably don't outweigh the disadvantages enough to tip the scales. This is because the advantages don't actually occur until the organization reaches a higher level of maturity. Keeping the disruptions to a minimum during the initial stages of establishing the PMCoE structure is the right thing to do.

Figure 1–3.   Project Manager Reporting Scenarios

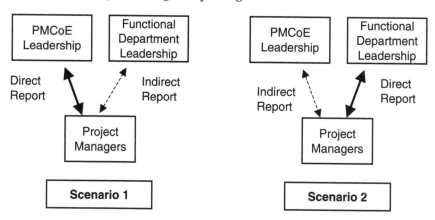

Table 1–3. Advantages and Disadvantages of Reporting Scenarios

Advantages	Disadvantages
• Facilitates synergy between and among managers • Provides more control over implementation of best practices • Facilitates transference of lessons learned and improvement of processes • Allows project managers to be dedicated to managing projects only	• Creates significant resistance from all participants • Does not change project managers' responsibilities initially • Removes subject matter experts from functional department control • Requires that project managers serve dual functions; not dedicated to projects only

PMCoE Organization Roles

Roles and staffing requirements vary depending upon the size, structure, support requirements, and average number of projects being managed concurrently within the various business units. Table 1–4 identifies roles, education, experience, and core capabilities that could be required within the various levels of the PMCoE structure. We do not suggest that all these positions be created, nor are they needed during the early stages of establishing the PMCoE organization structure. After the PMCoE organization structure is in place, staffing can be added as needed.

Summary

Companies choose to establish some form of centralized project management function within their organization structure for many different reasons. Understanding the driving forces and the motivations behind the creation of a project management center of excellence is important to know from the beginning. These project management functions may be called Project Office, Program Office, Project Support Office, or Project Management Center of Excellence. The number of levels (PMCOE – PMO – PSO – PO) typically depends on a number of variables. There is no one-size-fits-all

Table 1–4. PMCoE Organization Roles

Role	Education Experience Core Capabilities	PMCoE	PMO	PSO	PO	Functional Department
Functional Leader	Education: BS/MS + Project Management Professional (PMP) certification Experience: 10–12 years Core Capabilities: • Is experienced PM organization leader • Has expert knowledge of all PMBOK® Guide processes • Is influential in achieving fundamental change within the organization • Develops and maintains strategic relationships • Is skilled in PM mentoring and coaching	X	X	X		X
Senior Project Manager	Education: BS/MS + PMP Experience: 8–10 years Core Capabilities: • Directs and supervises project team • Has excellent communication skills • Has expert knowledge of PM processes • Is skilled in PM mentoring and coaching • Has large complex project experience • Has PM training experience	X	X	X	X	X
Project Coordinator	Education: BS/MS + PMP Experience: 8–10 years Core Capabilities: • Has mentoring and coaching skills • Has excellent communication skills		X	X	X	

continued

Table 1–4. *(Continued)*

Role	Education Experience Core Capabilities	PMCoE	PMO	PSO	PO	Functional Department
	• Has expert knowledge of PM processes • Has experience managing multiple projects					
Project Leader	Education: AS/BS/MS Experience: 1–3 years Core Capabilities: • Is a technical subject matter expert • Has good communication skills • Has conversant knowledge of PM processes • Has experience serving on project teams					X
Planning Analyst	Education: AS/BS/MS Experience: 5–7 years Core Capabilities: • Is expert in use of planning tools • Has strong analytical skills • Has expert knowledge of PM processes • Has experience managing multiple projects • Has teaching/training experience in planning	X	X	X		
Administrative Coordinator	Education: High School/AS Experience: 1–3 years Core Capabilities: • Requires minimum direction • Is proficient with PCs and office/PM applications • Has good communication skills • Is knowledgeable about PM processes	X	X	X	X	
Financial Administrator	Education: BS/MS Experience: 5–7 years	X	X			

Table 1–4. *(Continued)*

Role	Education Experience Core Capabilities	PMCoE	PMO	PSO	PO	Functional Department
	Core Capabilities: • Has expert knowledge of company financial systems • Has knowledge of PM processes • Has expert knowledge of earned value, NPV, and other cost analysis techniques					
Scheduler	Education: AS/BS Experience: 1–3 years Core Capabilities: • Is experienced in use of planning tools • Has multiple project planning experience • Has knowledge of PM processes			X	X	

model for creating a PMCoE. The methodology used to create them can be common to all; however, what they look like when completed will reflect similarities rather than an exact model.

The PMCoE is what this book is all about. Positioning the PMCoE within a company's structure makes a difference. The title given to the group does not matter as much. How the project management function is positioned can significantly affect its ability to accomplish its goals and objectives. If the goal is to institutionalize project management best practices throughout the enterprise, establishing a Project Management Center of Excellence at the highest level in the company is the first step to take. If the motivations are not compelling enough they will not convince the senior management team to move forward with an organizational change of this magnitude. Regardless of the size of the company, what you call the PMCoE is not as important as where it is positioned in the company, which will determine its level of autonomy and authority.

Institutionalizing project management requires a strong commitment and can typically require from three to five years of hard work to achieve. Those companies that stay the course and establish project management as a core competency are positioned to become world leaders, or at least to maintain their customers' recognition as world-class leaders in their respective industries. Establishing project management as a business function on the same level as the other typical functions of MIS, engineering, finance, marketing and sales is fundamental to effective building of a Project Management Center of Excellence. PMCoE organization structures and staffing roles can take many different forms.

Establishing a PMCoE is a strategic initiative that should be managed as a project by the highest level of the organization. The following chapters provide the steps involved in initiating, planning, executing, and closing a PMCoE implementation project.

CHAPTER 2

Initiating the PMCoE Project

Inaugurating an effective PMCoE, regardless of where it is positioned in the company, requires that some important steps be taken at the beginning. These steps improve the probability of success in the long term.

Assess Knowledge and Skill Levels

It is critical to determining the current conditions on any project before introducing a change that will impact how people do their work. Documenting the current conditions establishes a baseline from which to estimate the effort required to achieve the changes. Determining the effort is accomplished by measuring the gap between the *as is* (current conditions) and the *to be* (future conditions). The ability to measure progress toward achieving the change depends on having a clear understanding of baseline conditions.

The organization's current level of project management knowledge and skills (also referred to as maturity level) is the baseline that is established when implementing a PMCoE. Several processes are available to assess project management maturity. The following are three tools we have developed and used to determine the maturity of several organizations in recent years. (Examples of these three survey tools can be found in Appendix A as well as on the enclosed CD-ROM.)

1. **Management Team Survey** is a 33-question survey used to gather general information from department managers on communications and business environment issues that

can interfere with the implementation of project management best practices.

2. **Project Management Maturity Survey** is a set of 90 questions that covers all nine areas of the PMBOK® Guide. It is used to gather information from a sampling of people at the executive, functional, and operational levels of the organization in order to evaluate the organization's current knowledge and application of project management practices.

3. **Project Evaluation Survey** is used to evaluate 23 elements of project management processes, tools, templates, and forms. The survey tool can evaluate projects of different sizes, complexity, duration, including past projects as well as projects in progress. The primary objective is to analyze the amount and consistency of documentation among projects of various sizes, complexity, and duration. Another outcome is a validation or contradiction of current practices when compared to the Project Management Maturity Survey.

People in the organization often view surveys as an unjustified distraction and a waste of time, primarily because they feel the results do not provide much value to the participants. Planning and communication will help ensure willing participation, which in turn provides better data.

1. Start by defining the objectives for the survey information: what is needed, why is it needed, and what will be done with it. Provide this information in a meeting setting if possible to allow for questions and answers.

2. Determine how the survey results will be obtained (manually or electronically), how the participants will be selected, and how the results will be analyzed and communicated to the organization.

3. Prepare a plan for performing the survey by establishing a list of the participants. Develop a sign-up process to schedule participants' times, organize the meeting agendas, decide how to keep the participant responses anony-

mous, and determine how the results will be communicated back to the organization and survey participants.
4. Perform the survey(s), summarize the data, analyze the data, create a report, and communicate the results to the organization.

The value of a survey is only as good as the accuracy of the data collection and the proper interpretation of the responses. The interpretation should reflect the "average" conditions within the organization rather than the exceptions. Interpretation of the survey data requires an in-depth knowledge of the subject matter and an ability to express the findings in a clear and concise manner. The information obtained from the survey will help the PMCoE implementation team understand how significant the knowledge and skill level differences are across the organization. This in turn helps the team develop a more effective action plan for establishing the PMCoE and defines the type of services initially required. Once the assessment survey process is completed the next step is to acknowledge the PMCoE implementation project formally by issuing a project charter.

Writing a Charter

Writing the PMCoE charter is the most effective way to communicate what the PMCoE is all about. The PMCoE charter is designed to inform the organization of the purpose for creating the project Management Center of Excellence. It provides the "sizzle" that helps sell the idea to the organization. A charter also provides the means to formalize the creation of the PMCoE and serves to establish its role, responsibilities, accountability, and requisite authority. It includes the following information. (A sample charter can be found in Appendix A.)

- **Purpose:** explains why it is being created
- **Vision:** sets the standards for the Center of Excellence
- **Mission Statement:** defines its responsibilities
- **Strategy:** creates the proper environment

Figure 2–1. Creating a PMCoE Charter

- **Goals and Objectives:** explains achievements, defines success
- **Methodology:** defines strategies used to achieve excellence
- **Critical Success Factors (CSF):** identifies risks to success
- **Span of control:** PMCoE roles, responsibilities, accountability, and authority

Presenting the PMCoE charter to the executive management team to review, approve, formally adopt, and sign must occur before proceeding. Moving ahead without executive management support and approval is a risky move that will probably lose the game. Once the management team adopts the charter, it should be presented to the entire organization as part of the communication process in the initiation phase. Figure 2–1 identifies the key elements of an effective charter.

Writing a Scope Statement

One of the first activities that should be undertaken when projects are started is documenting the Scope Of Work (SOW). Defining the work that is included in a project as well as specific work that will not be included is critical to the successful completion of the project. The SOW is contained in a document referred to as a Statement of Work, which typically contains the following elements (a sample is included in Appendix B):

- Project name
- Project identification number
- Project sponsor or champion
- Project manager assigned to the project
- List of project stakeholder representatives
- List of project team members
- List of steering (management oversight) team members
- Description of corporate strategic objective driving the project
- Description of the project purpose
- List of sponsor and stakeholder expectations
- Description of how the project will achieve the stated purpose
- List of business benefits with defined validation measures
- List of special requirements (equipment, skills, knowledge, etc.)
- List of specific inclusions
- List of specific exclusions
- List of project deliverables
- List of project constraints
- List of project assumptions
- List of project critical success factors
- Preliminary project budget
- Preliminary project milestones
- Proposed readiness review date

Preparing a scope statement that includes this level of detail is necessary for strategic, mission-critical projects, and creating them can require a significant amount of time. Unfortunately, scope statements of this magnitude are rarely done, which is one of the primary causes of project failures. The lack of good project preparation is typically caused by pressures placed on the project manager to get started on the work of the project in order to meet deadlines imposed by management or the customer. Communicating the information contained within the project charter and the project scope statement to the project team and its stakeholders is an important next step. Holding a project kick-off meeting, especially for strategic initiatives implementing a PMCoE, is an ideal way to distribute this important communication.

Assembling Project and Steering Teams

Selecting and securing commitment for project team members who have a significant level of skills and experience needed to complete the project successfully is essential. The task is usually not an easy one, particularly on projects affecting most of the functional areas of the company. Functional managers are typically reluctant to assign their key people—especially to long-term projects. Securing these representatives is a critical success factor of the project.

A project steering team is typically comprised of company executives and department managers serving in an oversight capacity. The team is needed to perform the following functions:

- Provide corporate leadership direction
- Review project progress
- Remove roadblocks that prevent progress
- Review and approve proposed changes to project scope, cost, and schedule
- Hold the project team accountable for on-time and within-budget project completion
- Recognize and reward performance

Getting the commitment of company executives and department manages to serve on the project steering team is another critical success factor for mission-critical projects.

Once the charter, scope statement, project team, and steering team have been assembled the next step is to start the project by getting everyone on the same page.

Hold a Kick-off Event

Building a PMCoE is creating a new business function, which is a big deal and should be treated as such. Among the many different ways to publicize the creation of the PMCoE are:

- A story with interviews in the company newsletter
- Posters and intranet Web site announcements
- Creation of a PMCoE intranet Web site
- Visits to department team meetings by the PMCoE leader
- A company-wide e-mail announcement
- Multiple announcements for Q&A events held at all company locations
- Special, by-invitation-only kick-off event (typically limited to executives, department managers, supervisors, project managers, and special guests from all areas of the company)

Doing all or most of these ideas provides the most effective means to ensure a successful PMCoE launch, because they provide multiple opportunities to communicate important information to all levels of the organization. The underlying agenda for each should be the same.

1. Identify the organizational position, roles, and responsibilities
2. Define the purpose, vision, mission, goals, and objectives
3. Identify the positive effects and benefits it will produce
4. Reduce resistance through frequent and varied communication methods
5. Provide answers to FAQs (frequently asked questions)

Delivering important messages repeatedly in a variety of ways can ensure the intended audience will receive and understand them. Planning communications is an important aspect of managing most projects, and it is critical to successfully establishing a PMCoE. It is particularly important when it comes to communicating with company executives, managers, supervisors, and project managers. The messages should be tailored in style and content for the specific audience, because each has different communication requirements.

Holding a by-invitation-only kick-off event is a critical activity that can directly affect the time it takes to successfully implement project management disciplines across the organization. This event can provide the means to:

- Give visibility to corporate executive commitment and support
- Establish a level playing field of project management knowledge
- Present the PMCoE vision, mission, goals and objectives
- Present a PMCoE implementation plan
- Engage functional managers in a hands-on participation of the PMCoE implementation
- Establish an in-house knowledge network to facilitate a forum for learning

Developing the kick-off event begins with the preparation of a proposal to sell senior management on the value of holding a special event, to request their active participation, and to obtain approval for the event budget at the level required. The proposal should include the following information.

- An explanation of why the event should be held and the benefits that will be achieved
- The proposed event theme and activities to be included
- A list of potential external speaker(s) with presentation content
- A list of desired internal speakers with anticipated roles and responsibilities
- The proposed event location (in house or off site), preliminary date, and timing information
- A description of handouts/gifts (books, bound notepads, puzzles, etc.) to be distributed to attendees as event mementos
- The event budget

Once the initial approvals have been obtained, you can use the following steps to plan the event.

1. Finalize the theme, agenda, and event activity details.
2. Establish the location, date, and time; visit the facilities to confirm suitability and review requirements with facilities staff coordinator.
3. Identify and obtain commitment of internal and external speakers and set up a date for delivery of presentations and handouts; confirm all speakers two weeks before the event.
4. Finalize the list of attendees, send out personal invitations (include a message from the CEO/president encouraging their attendance—it is very effective) two months in advance, and follow up with details and a reminder two weeks before the event.
5. Arrange for facilities, food, handouts, transportation, and lodging for guest speaker(s).
6. Finalize the event memento handouts/gifts and make arrangements to receive them well in advance of the event.
7. Hold the event and have fun!
8. Follow up with notes of appreciation and acknowledgments to speakers and all attendees.

Table 2–1 shows a kick-off meeting agenda we have used for two major PMCoE kick-off events, both of which were highly successful.

The focus of the morning session is to create a level playing field by presenting an overview of what the profession of project management is, where it came from, what benefits it provides, how it is viewed in the marketplace today, and where is it going as a profession in the future. A well-known speaker who is recognized as a project management subject matter expert should deliver this message. Beginning the day with opening remarks provides an opportunity for organization leaders to welcome participants, recognize important guests, and most importantly

Table 2–1. Kick-off Meeting Agenda

Morning Session	30 minutes	Registration and continental breakfast
	30 minutes	Opening remarks and introductions
	3 hours with 15 min. break at 9:30 a.m.	Keynote speaker—What is project management, where did it come from, what are the benefits, and where is it going as a profession?
	1 hour	Lunch break
Afternoon Session	2 hours	PMCoE presentation: charter and creation of a PM Forum (internal network)
	30 minutes	Wrap-up Q&A

voice their commitment to, and stress the importance of, everyone's support of the PMCoE organization implementation.

The afternoon session focuses on presenting the PMCoE charter and introducing a concept for creating an internal knowledge network to provide a forum to discuss and share project management issues, successes, failures, and lessons learned on a periodic basis. Knowledge networks would be established at the PMCoE and PSO level of the company with membership comprising department managers, project managers, and invited guests. Meetings are typically held on a quarterly basis.

Create Task Force Teams

Engaging the functional department managers as active participants in creating, developing, and promoting ongoing activities of the PMCoE is a critical step in the process of building an effective PMCoE. Including these managers also helps the process of instilling project management best practices across the organization as a core competency. One way to accomplish this is to create task force teams responsible for assisting the PMCoE in the development, management, and continuous improvement of the processes, procedures, tools, and templates. Organizations have created task force teams in Authorization, Standards, Education, and Readiness, four key areas that directly affect a timely adoption of project management best practices.

Tables 2–2 through 2–5 are partial scope statements developed for each of the task force teams. They include the purpose, expectations, and benefits for each.

Four Key PMCoE Elements

We believe the key to successfully executing project management best practices across an organization depends on implanting the four functions that are the key elements of an effective Project Management Center of Excellence.

Table 2–2. Authorization Task Force Team Scope

Purpose	Establish a project authorization process to ensure the uses of resources are in alignment with corporate strategic goals and objectives. It addresses the following issues: • Project identification • Project categorization • Project prioritization • Project portfolio management • Project request review • Master planning and capital budget The ATF develops the policies, procedures, tools, and templates required to achieve the stated purpose and to satisfy corporate expectations.
Expectations	• Provide a means to identify and manage all projects. • Improve ability to effectively manage and allocate resources. • Provide the means to ensure all projects are aligned with and support corporate goals and objectives. • Provide a means to track actual vs. budgeted project costs.
Business Benefits	• Improves master planning and capital budget planning processes • Provides an enterprise-wide forecast of future projects • Facilitates the growth of the organization's project management maturity

Table 2–3.   Standards Task Force Team

Purpose	Establish project management standards and methods to be applied to all projects. The team assists the PMCoE in the development, maintenance, and subsequent changes to the following: • Policies • Procedures • Processes • Tools and templates The STF develops the policies, procedures, tools, and templates required to achieve the stated purpose and to satisfy corporate expectations.
Expectations	• Provide a standard methodology for managing projects enterprise-wide. • Provide standard processes, tools, and templates for managing projects.
Business Benefits	• Improves efficiency and shortens the learning curve • Reduces project timing and cost • Improves project organization, planning, and management skills • Enables tracking of actual vs. budgeted project costs • Facilitates regular management review of project status • Aids the growth of the organization's project management maturity

Authorization   Authorization is the formal process for developing a forecast plan that identifies corporate goals and objectives. This in turn is translated into a list of prioritized projects documented as the organization's portfolio of projects. It includes a formal review and approval process to ensure that company resources (money and people) are distributed only to authorized projects that directly support corporate goals and objectives. A process to adjust the approved portfolio of projects for new opportunities during the calendar year of the plan is also included.

Standards   Standards is the formal acceptance of guidelines that define common processes, tools, templates, and technology. These guidelines are to be used consistently across the organization to manage all authorized projects.

Table 2–4. Education Task Force Team

Purpose	Develop a comprehensive education and training program to enable the organization to embrace and effectively apply the project management standards consistently and to achieve improvements on a continuous basis. Establish: • Education and training goals • Education and training requirements • Education and training curriculum The ETF develops the policies, procedures, tools, and templates required to achieve the stated purpose and to satisfy corporate expectations.
Expectations	• Provide a comprehensive education and training program that effectively distributes project management knowledge and skills enterprise-wide. • Provide an internal qualification and certification program for project managers. • Provide education and training opportunities in project management at all levels of the organization.
Business Benefits	• Improves time-to-market, quality-to-market, and cost-to-market • Reduces project timing and cost • Improves project organization, planning, and management skills • Aids the growth of the organization's project management maturity

Table 2–5. Readiness Task Force Team

Purpose	Establish a project readiness check process to evaluate a project's "preparedness" to proceed prior to project start-up. The RTF develops policies, procedures, tools, and templates required to achieve the stated purpose and to satisfy corporate expectations.
Expectations	Provide a means to enable projects to be successful.
Business Benefits	• Ensures project standards are being properly applied to all projects • Facilitates creation of a "learning organization" environment • Aids the growth of the organization's project management maturity

Figure 2–2.   The Four Critical Elements

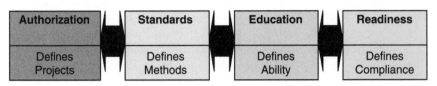

Education   Education includes the development and delivery of programs to provide the knowledge, skills, and capabilities required at all levels of the organization to effectively apply the standards in the management of all authorized projects.

Readiness   Readiness refers to the formal processes that ensure and validate that the required standards, knowledge, and skills are present prior to project start-up; that work in-process is meeting project deliverables; and that post-project reviews, including documentation of lessons learned, are carried out to help ensure the success of all authorized projects. Readiness also means that continuous improvement of authorization, standards, education, and readiness elements occur in a timely fashion.

Summary

Determining the effort required to implement the changes necessary to satisfy PMCoE implementation goals and objectives demands a clear analysis of the gap between current conditions and those that are desired. Several tools for assessing current project management knowledge and practices were discussed in this chapter.

Creating a charter, developing the scope statement, assembling the project and steering teams are all important first steps in the process of initiating projects. Charters provide the formal acknowledgement that a project has been approved. The project scope statement defines the who, what, why, when, and how of the project. It creates the vision to meet standards of excellence, documents the goals and objectives to achieve success, and defines roles, responsibilities, accountability and authority. Establishing a

PMCoE should be treated as a strategic initiative, and as such creating a project steering team is a critical first step that can affect the final outcome.

Effective communication is critical in the beginning stages of most projects, and that is especially true for strategic initiatives that will affect the whole company. Project kick-off meetings provide an excellent opportunity for management to communicate the importance of the initiative by visibly showing their commitment and support for the project. Project kick-off meetings can help remove potential resistance for the project that is typically caused by lack of information. Kick-off meetings provide an excellent opportunity to involve project stakeholders such as executives, department managers, project managers, and other staff members who will be key players in the PMCoE implementation process. One of the ways presented in this chapter to involve project stakeholders is having executive management assign them to a task force team. Task force teams are responsible for developing the policies, processes, procedures, tools, and templates for project authorization, standards, education and readiness. Active participation in task force teams creates ownership in the project, which in turn reduces or eliminates resistance to changes required to achieve project goals and objectives.

Establishing a formalized strategic forecast planning process that identifies corporate goals and objectives and puts a project portfolio management process into place to achieve them is the next step.

CHAPTER 3

Creating and Managing a Project Portfolio

Every journey begins with a destination, or it should, because without a predetermined destination you would not know that you have arrived. We are all on a journey through life, and those who plan their journeys with milestones of accomplishments (goals and objectives) are typically those who are most successful in completing each leg of their journey. World-class industry leaders are those organizations that set high goals and objectives and develop plans to achieve them. This chapter is about leveraging limited resources to ensure they are used effectively to achieve corporate goals and objectives.

Identifying Organizational Goals and Objectives

Having limited resources (people and money) is an aspect of business common to every organization. The challenge most of them share is distributing those resources effectively to achieve the highest return on their investment. You would think that identifying organizational goals and objectives would be an obvious requirement, however, that is not the case for many organizations. In many cases, if it is being done, it is not done very well. There are many reasons why this effort is ignored or done poorly.

- There is no formal process to define corporate goals and objectives.
- Firefighting diverts attention from long-range planning.

- Stated goals and objectives are not qualified or quantifiable.
- The development of corporate goals and objectives stops at the top.
- There is no formal measurement process to validate status.
- Accountability to achieve goals does not exist.
- There is no personal reward for achieving goals nor penalty for failing to achieve them.
- Achieving goals fails to produce desired results.

Defining company goals must start at the top and cascade down through the organization structure to the individual department manager's goals and objectives. The goals and objectives at each level of the organization should support the corporate goals and objectives as well as the goals and objectives of the level it reports to. Establishing goals and objectives is a forecasting activity that requires significant planning and training to achieve the results intended. A formalized process must be documented that identifies the steps taken, roles and responsibilities defined, and the training provided at all levels of the organization.

Achieving Corporate Goals and Objectives

Companies of all sizes use many methods and techniques with varying degrees of success. There is, however, a simple but effective method used by the Donnelly Corporation, a leading automotive supplier of interior and exterior mirrors with headquarters in Holland, Michigan. Dwane Baumgardner, chairman and CEO of Donnelly Corporation, wrote a paper entitled, "A Constant State of Becoming: Management by Planning at Donnelly Corporation," published by GOAL/QPC in 1998. This paper discusses the process, developed by Donnelly, called Management by Planning (MBP). Mr. Baumgardner presents the purpose and value of the MBP process in the paper's introduction.

We are all in a constant state of *becoming*, which will happen either by design or by default. I believe that terms and management fads like *change management,* or *corporate renewal,* or *reengineering* often misdirect thinking and action on a principal reality of life—all life is change, and we are in a constant state of becoming. The reason I believe these management fads are misdirecting is that many of them present change as an event, a single project or series of discreet projects each with its own finish line. On the contrary, I have found change to be a highly systemic and neverending process. The good news is that we have the advantage today of being able to manage our becoming. Pity the dinosaurs who were victims of changes; and I'm not just talking about T-Rex. How about Studabaker, Packard, canal builders, railroads, and the A&P grocery stores? We now have a much greater opportunity to control our own futures, to be actors not victims, to become by design not default.

This article is about how our company thinks and acts on our commitment to continuous growth and performance, and a most effective process for managing our becoming, what we call Management by Planning (MBP).

Baumgardner goes on to state that the company's operating philosophy is based on a partnership among five constituents: customers, owners, employees, suppliers, and the community they live in. The MBP process is designed to identify goals and objectives to achieve improvements in each of the five areas, which in turn result in helping the company become a world-class leader in its industry.

Baumgardner tells us in his paper "MBP is based on the Japanese system known as *hoshin kanri,* which owes a debt of gratitude to Shewhart and Deming." He goes on to state "I won't kid you and tell you that we are doing it perfectly. This process is also in a state of becoming. However, as a process, it holds tremendous capacity to manage our growth, involve all our people, and produce results that exceed the expectations of all our constituents."

The Donnelly MBP process is an excellent methodology for identifying an organization's goals and objectives. It even has an element that identifies the "action items" to be taken in the course of achieving the stated goals and objectives. In my opinion, the MBP is an excellent methodology for defining worthy goals and objectives, but stops short by not developing a portfolio of projects to ensure those "action items" are properly managed.

Hosin Kanri

The following information about the origins of *hoshin kanri* was extracted from the *Hoshin Handbook, Second Edition* (ISBN #0-9651861-0-5) written by Pete Babich, President, Total Quality Engineering, Inc. (http://www.tqe.com) and reprinted here with his permission.

> *Hoshin kanri* was developed in Japan to communicate company policy to everyone in the organization. *Hoshin's* primary benefit is to focus activity on the key things necessary for success. Japanese Deming Prize winners credit *hoshin* as being a key contributor to their business success. Progressive U.S. companies, such as Hewlett-Packard and Xerox, have also adopted *hoshin* as their strategic planning process. *Hoshin* meets the intent of the Malcolm Baldrige National Quality Award criteria for planning. Simply put, *hoshin* is a system of forms and rules that encourages employees to analyze situations, create plans for improvement, conduct performance checks, and take appropriate action.
> Deming had made a previous visit to Japan in 1947 as part of an economic survey mission. Japanese and government officials were already familiar with him; therefore, the Japanese Union of Scientists and Engineers (JUSE) asked Deming to provide the expert training. During a two-month period in June 1950, Deming trained hundreds of engineers, managers, and scholars. He also conducted a session for top management. Deming's lec-

tures focused on three key areas: the use of the PDCA (Plan-Do-Check-Action) cycle, the importance of understanding the causes of variation, and process control through the use of control charts.

Through Deming's training and JUSE's subsequent training, Japan began a major effort to improve quality by implementing statistical quality control (SQC). Initial results were positive, but Japan entered a period of overemphasis on SQC. Engineers continued to push SQC, but workers resisted, data collection techniques were inadequate, and top management did not show much interest. In 1954, JUSE invited Joseph M. Juran to lecture on management's role in promoting quality control activities. Juran's visit marked a turning point in Japan's quality maturity. It shifted from primarily dealing with technology to an overall concern for total quality management.

Juran pointed out that it was management's responsibility to lead quality improvement efforts. A key element of that responsibility was to define the quality policy and ensure that everyone understood and supported it. Management saw the company's planning process as the vehicle to fulfill its responsibility for quality management. At about the same time as Juran's visit, Peter Drucker's book, *The Practice of Management,* which described the concepts of management by objectives (MBO), was published in Japanese.

The Japanese blended Deming and Juran's teachings with the concepts of MBO and began their first attempts at strategic quality planning. Each individual company created its own planning processes. The Deming Application Prize shared best planning practices, and common themes began to appear. In 1957, Kaoru Ishikawa published a paper stressing the importance of management and operational policies. Juran made another visit to Japan in 1960, emphasizing the responsibility of management for setting goals and planning for improvement.

Japanese planning techniques continued to evolve and improve. In 1965, Bridgestone Tire published a report analyzing the planning techniques used by Deming prizewinning companies. The techniques described were given the name *hoshin kanri*. By 1975, *hoshin* was widely accepted in Japan.

Hoshin began to creep into the United States in the early 80s. This occurred mainly because some U.S. companies had divisions or subsidiaries in Japan that were Deming prizewinners. The winning companies include Hewlett-Packard's YHP Division, Fuji-Xerox, and Texas Instrument's Oita plant. Other U.S. companies, including Florida Power and Light, searched for Japanese companies in their industries.

Understanding the origin of the words can provide insight into *hoshin* concepts. The term *hoshin* is short for *hoshin kanri*. The word *hoshin* can be broken into two parts. The literal translation of ho is "direction." The literal translation of shin is "needle," so the word *hoshin* could translate as "direction needle" or the English equivalent of "compass." The word *kanri* can also be broken into two parts. The first part, *kan*, translates as "control" or "channeling." The second part, ri, translates as "reason" or "logic." Taken altogether, *hoshin kanri* means management and control of the company's direction needle or focus.

方針 *hoshin* = a course, a policy, a plan, an aim

管理 *kanri* = administration, management, control, charge of, care for

The most popular English translation for *hoshin* is Policy Deployment, the term used in most books by American authors. No matter what you call it, however, *hoshin* is effective and helps organizations become more competitive.*

---

*Pete Babich, *Hoshin Handbook, Second Edition* (Total Quality Engineering, Inc., pp. 17–19, 1996)

Donnelly developed a simple process using the *hoshin kanri* concept to document its MBP goals and objectives. Figure 3–1, management by planning format, shows the primary format used by Donnelly.

Donnelly developed an Excel spreadsheet application they used at all levels of the company for its managing by planning process. The spreadsheet was divided into six sections that contained cells with the following information:

- Section 1—contains the name of the business unit leader and a pentagon shape signifying the corporate goals and objectives these five categories would address.
- Section 2—lists the corporate goals and objectives vertically, one per column.
- Section 3—contains a list of the business unit's goals and objectives that supported the corporate goals and objectives.
- Section 4—contains a matrix of rows and columns containing Xs, which indicated the connections between one or more corporate and business unit goals and objectives.
- Section 5—contains a list of actions that support one or more business goals and objectives.
- Section 6—contains a matrix of rows and columns containing Xs, which indicated the connections between one or more business unit goals and objectives and supporting actions.

Figure 3–1. Management by Planning Form

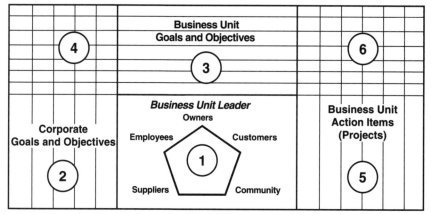

The spreadsheet application also includes separate worksheets for each business unit, which contain baseline vs. actual measurements that track monthly progress towards achieving the numerical goal identified for each item listed in section 3. Summary worksheets are also included in the application to provide running cumulative totals for all of the items listed in section 3.

Establish Project Portfolios

Creating a project portfolio is part of the forecasting process. It involves developing a list of projects that directly support achieving a business unit's goals and objectives. The corporate project portfolio is a combination of the project portfolios created within the various departments of the company, starting with a corporate project list and extending down through the organization structure to the department level.

Compilation of all these lists into a master project portfolio ensures that duplications are eliminated and that projects with similar or competing goals and objectives are identified. In a large organization this can become a daunting task, especially if a single source with overall responsibility is not established. One of the roles of the PMCoE is to manage this task, which is of extreme importance to the strategic distribution of the company's limited resources.

The process of developing a project portfolio begins at each level of the organization after the MBP process has been completed. Each unit is responsible for creating its own portfolio of projects, which in turn is summarized and combined with the level above. Once again this task could become overwhelming in a large organization if a PMCoE organization structure were not in place. One of the benefits of developing and maintaining the project portfolios at all levels is that over time it will help the organization improve its ability to understand its capability and capacity to manage work. Having the ability to quantify the company's resource capability and capacity to manage projects is a necessary ingredient for creating the forecast project portfolio and capital budget plan. Establishing the corporate and business unit goals and objectives should be based on a quantifiable knowledge of the company's resource capacity and capability to ensure the goals and objectives can be reasonably achieved.

Capacity and Capability

Most organizations determine their capacity and capability to produce goods or services with a relative amount of confidence. However, estimating their capacity and capability to manage work in the form of projects is another issue altogether. Determining work capacity and capability is an extremely difficult but important task that is a critical prerequisite to effectively managing the resources of the company. The following systems must be in place to accurately determine capacity and capability:

- A standard time recording and reporting system
- Documentation of workers' skills and knowledge
- Project estimating standards
- A project portfolio management system

Standard Time Recording   This is a basic requirement for developing accurate estimates of the effort it takes to complete various activities. Accurate estimates are often based on historical information, which can only be obtained by keeping accurate and timely records. Efficiency and productivity cannot be accurately measured and therefore improved without documenting work effort. Implementing time recording and reporting systems in business areas is usually a hard sell and is met with a high degree of resistance. Office employees consider their work to be more flexible and varied with less dependence on specific process regimens, unlike machine or assembly operations in the factory setting. Changing this mindset is not easy, but it is an absolute requirement for process improvements, both in the office as well as the manufacturing areas.

Workers' Skills and Knowledge   Documenting the skills and technical or special knowledge of the workers throughout the organization is needed to determine an organization's capacity and capability to perform work. Gathering information concerning employee skills and knowledge is typically done during the hiring process and the information is held and managed by the human resources department. Skills management has recently become a specialized field with many of its aspects incorporated into human resources electronic applications, such as PeopleSoft. Using computerized systems allows data to be accessed securely by department managers and others who have been authorized to do so. Skills and knowledge databases can be used to create resource pools, which in turn can be used to plan multiple projects not only within departments, but also across the entire company. Establishing the initial skills and knowledge database is a significant project, which is one of the reasons why few organizations undertake the effort. Those that do, however, realize considerable returns on the time and cost they have invested by improving their:

- Ability to quickly match skills and knowledge with requirements
- Ability to schedule multiple projects requiring shared resources
- Likelihood of transferring critical knowledge
- Identification and use of subject matter experts
- Ability to manage critical resources
- Identification of missing resources, under- or over-utilized resources, and under- or over-staffed departments
- Creation and management of resource pools

Project Estimating Standards   Developing accurate estimates for customer quotations and projects is an important step in the process of winning new business and completing projects on time and within budget. Keeping accurate records on all projects provides a historical record on which to base future estimates. Any number of important metrics can be recorded on most projects. The following are typically the most important:

- Actual versus estimated effort to complete project tasks
- Number of issues submitted with average time to resolution
- Number of changes requested versus number approved and average time required to process to resolution
- Number of schedule variances (early/late) reported during each phase of the project (initiation, planning, execution, and closing) with average duration of the variances

Figure 3–2. Project Actual vs. Baseline Plan

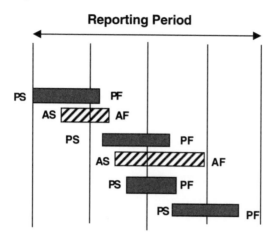

Reporting Period

Performance Index Calculations

Reporting Period	PS	AS	PF	AF	Total PSF	Total ASF	Performance Index
dd/mm/yy -dd/mm/yy	4	2	4	2	8	4	.50

John Goodpasture and Jim Sumara devised a methodology for measuring project performance that they presented in a paper entitled "Time Centric Earned Value—The Next Generation." The methodology has some very simple rules and a criterion to analyze planned versus actual schedule starts and finishes. It is illustrated in Figure 3–2.

Simple Rules

- Rule 1: A task is either *scheduled* or not
- Rule 2: A *scheduled* task is either started, finished, or not (There is no partial credit.)

Criteria for Claiming Progress

- Task Start: Predecessor tasks are completed, task is staffed, resources are in place, and meaningful effort has begun. Valued as (1) when these conditions are met; (0) when not.
- Task Finish: Task has completed scope; scheduled successors can begin. Valued as (1) when conditions are met; (0) when not.
  (Recap: Start = 1, Finish = 1, Everything else = 0)

Recognizing Time Performance

- *Planned* Starts (PS) and *Planned* Finishes (PF) = (1) credit for each planned start + (1) credit for each planned finish in the reporting period
- *Actual* Starts (AS) and *Actual* Finishes (AF) = (1) credit for each actual start + (1) credit for each actual finish in the actual finish reporting period
- Task Performance Index (TPI_{month}) = Sum of *actuals* divided by *planned* for the reporting period
- Task Performance Index (TPI_{cum}) = Cumulative of *actuals* divided by *planned* for the project to date

Project Portfolio Management System   A documented process must be established to provide a means to identify projects that have been approved versus those that have not. The key elements of a project portfolio management system are:

- Authorization Team, comprising PMCoE and business unit leaders, established at whatever levels the project portfolio lists have been set up for; responsible for reviewing and approving projects to proceed
- Project Submittal Requirements
  - Project summary, including its purpose, description, deliverables, and benefits
  - Preliminary milestone schedule
  - Proposed budget with capital and expense items detailed
  - Cost benefit analysis (NPV, RRI, ROI, projected cost-saving benefits)

- Resource requirements
- Management Project Reviews: project status reviews held monthly for senior management at each business unit level

Our experience indicates that few companies are very good at getting a handle on their capability and capacity to manage multiple projects. This is largely because they may be doing *some* of the things noted above, but not *all* of them, and all of them are necessary to do an adequate job. The result is usually that expectations for projects to be completed on time and within budget are often not met because the ability to judge capacity and capability to deliver are inadequate.

Implementing an MBP or similar process and creating a master project portfolio helps quantify the work that needs to be done in order to achieve goals and objectives. By themselves, however, they do not validate the organization's capacity and capability to complete the work within the confines of the fiscal year plan.

The Project Portfolio and Capital Budget Plan

A sample project portfolio and capital budget plan process are shown in Figure 3–3, Table 3–1, and Table 3–2. This process is used as a strategic planning process (SPP) in conjunction with the MBP process as a generic process adaptable to any organization.

Creating a master list of projects takes lots of work the first time, but becomes easier, like most new processes, the more times it is done. The benefits of creating and maintaining the project portfolio will quickly become evident to the executives and managers who have the responsibility to manage the resources assigned to them.

- Projects are prioritized, making resource planning easier
- Planning department resource requirements becomes easier with fewer changes
- Coordination of resources between departments becomes easier
- Project scheduling becomes more reliable
- More projects are completed on time and within budget

Figure 3–3. Strategic Forecast Plan Process

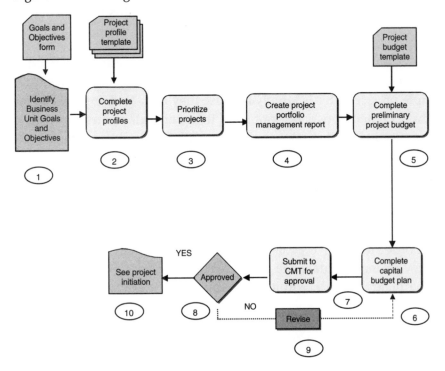

Effectively managing resources is usually high on every manager's list, and projects typically account for a large segment of the work done in most office departments.

New Opportunities

A formal process must be created to manage new opportunities as they arise during the master plan's fiscal year. Figure 3–4 and Table 3–3 provide an example of such a process.

Managing the Project Portfolio

Visibility and ready access to information regarding projects in progress are two important aspects of managing the portfolio. A

Table 3–1. Process Step Description: Strategic Forecast Plan

Step	Step Definition	Role(s)	Activity Definition
1	Identify Business Unit Goals and Objectives	Management Team	The management team identifies and documents the business unit's annual goals and objectives.
2	Complete Project Profiles	Managers	Managers identify projects required to satisfy the business unit goals and objectives. A project profile form is completed for each proposed project and filed with the PMCoE for future reference.
3	Prioritize Projects	Management Team	The management team determines the prioritization of the proposed projects for the plan year, thereby creating the input for the project portfolio management report.
4	Create Project Portfolio Management Report	PMCoE	The PMCoE compiles a list of proposed projects and produces a forecasted project portfolio management report for the plan year.
5	Complete Preliminary Project Budget	Managers	Managers complete preliminary budgets for each proposed project. A template is used to develop this preliminary budget and a copy is filed with the PMCoE for future reference.
6	Create Project Capital Budget Plan	Management Team	The proposed project estimated budgets are summarized to create a project capital budget plan for the plan year.
7	Submit to CMT for Approval	PMCoE	The proposed master project capital budget plan and project portfolio management report are submitted to the corporate management team (CMT) for review and approval.
8	CMT Review/Approval	CMT	The CMT reviews the proposed project capital budget plan and approves it or requests revisions.
9	Revise	CMT	If required, the revised report is resubmitted until it obtains final approval.
10	See Project Initiation	Management	Once approved, the project proceeds with the project initiation process.

Table 3–2. RRAA Matrix: Strategic Forecast Plan

Role	Responsibility	Accountability	Authority
Organization's Senior Executive	Provides leadership direction and supports the management team in annual implementation of the strategic forecast planning and capital budget development process	Facilitates the process that prioritizes projects and develops the project capital budget plan	Requires adjustments to the approved project prioritization as circumstances dictate and provides final approval for all organization projects
Functional Department Managers	Participate in the annual strategic forecast planning process, identify projects to satisfy goals and objectives, prepare preliminary budget for all proposed projects	Review, commit to, and support the project portfolio list and the master project capital budget plan prior to CMT review and approval	Request revisions to the project portfolio list and the project capital budget plan prior to its being submitted to the CMT for approval
PMCoE	Assigns a classification level to each proposed project and prepares the project portfolio list using the prioritized list developed by the management team	Assists the functional managers in developing their individual proposed project plans	Develops, maintains, distributes, and helps implement the project portfolio development process and facilitates the annual implementation in a timely manner
Corporate Management Team (CMT)	Provides leadership to the organization by establishing clear vision, mission, objectives, and goals through the strategic planning process	Reviews and approves the organization's strategic planning process plan and FY project capital budget plan for the coming year in a timely manner	Accepts, requests revisions, or specifies exceptions prior to approving the plan

Figure 3–4. Project Request/Authorization Process

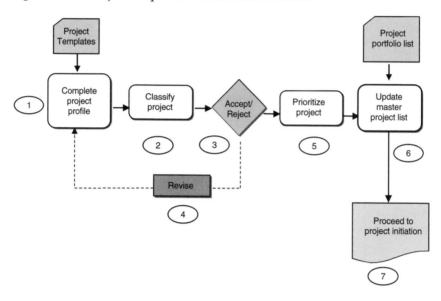

master project list in a table format that contains the following information is an easy but effective system to create and maintain.

- ID#—Identification number assigned to each approved project
- Name—Short name by which the project will be known
- DEPT—Department manager who owns the project
- PM—Project manager or team leader assigned to the project
- SD—Start date (P-dd/mm = planned, A-dd/mm = actual)
- ED—End date (P-dd/mm = planned, A-dd/mm = actual)
- SIZ—Estimated duration of the project in months
- PHZ—Current phase the project is in (INT = initiation, PLN = planning, EXC = execution, CLS = closing)
- STAT—Current status of the project (color coded: green = on schedule, yellow = potential for variance, red = overdue)
- CAL—12 monthly columns with plan colored light blue and progress colored black)

See the template PMMG 1.11 in Appendix B for an example.

Table 3-3. Process Step Description: Project Request/Authorization Process

Step	Step Definition	Role(s)	Activity Definition
1	Complete Project Profile	Functional Manager	After determining that a business opportunity requires a project to fulfill a business need, the manager completes these documents and submits them to the PMCoE.
2	Classify Project	PMCoE	The PMCoE assigns a classification level to the project.
3	Accept/Reject	Project Authorization Team (PAT)	The PAT reviews, approves or requests additional information, or rejects the project. If the project is rejected, the PAT provides the manager with justification for this business decision.
4	Revise	Functional Manager	The manager provides additional information and revises the project summary and/or project milestone plan as required. If the PAT rejects the project, the manager communicates this to the intended project sponsor and customer.
5	Prioritize Project	Project Authorization Team	If the project is approved, the team establishes a priority for the project and determines how the master project portfolio list will be adjusted to accommodate this new project.
6	Update Master Project List	PMCoE	The PMCoE updates the master project portfolio list to include the new project and makes other adjustments as directed by the PAT.
7	Proceed to Project Initiation	Functional Manager	The manager follows the Project Initiation Process when the time arrives to start the initiation phase of the project.

There are many ways to provide access to this kind of information:

- Maintain the table in an electronic file on the LAN/WAN system with access determined by the system administrator.
- Post the information on an Internet Web site created and maintained by the PMCoE.
- Provide the information through a "dashboard" feature available from several software vendors.

A monthly management review of projects is another important method of providing visibility. It also facilitates the update of the master project list. Monthly reviews with the managers of the business units facilitate communications among managers concerning project status and create a heightened awareness of critical issues. The fundamental requirements for successful monthly project reviews include the following rules.

- Manager attendance is mandatory. If a schedule conflict occurs, a delegate represents the department.
- Project managers present the project status, if possible. If not, a team delegate represents the project manager.
- Project status is based on the progress since the previous report.
- Projects are reviewed in four categories: (1) new projects, (2) projects in-progress, (3) completed projects, and (4) future projects. The following details should be reported:

1. **New projects** (those that have started since the previous report)
   - ✓ Scope of work is reviewed
   - ✓ Overview of project schedule
   - ✓ Major project risks
   - ✓ Anticipated benefits
2. **Projects in-progress**
   - ✓ Current status (green = on time, yellow = running late, red = overdue)

Table 3–4. RRAA Matrix: Project Request/Authorization Process

Role	Responsibility	Accountability	Authority
Functional Department Manager	Identifies business opportunities that require new projects, gathers requirements. Prepares a project profile and submits it to the Authorization Team for review and approval. Informs the project customer and sponsor of project approval or provides the PAT justification if it is rejected	Completes the proposed project profile document with sufficient detail to allow proper classification and review by the PAT	Requests requirements from proposed project customers and sponsors to establish compelling justification for the project
PMCoE	Serves on the PAT and updates the master project portfolio list with new approved projects Assigns a classification level to new projects	Provides reasoning to support project classification if requested Establishes and maintains master project portfolio list files	Establishes and refines project classification level criteria as experience is gained over time
Project Authorization Team	Reviews and approves proposed projects to be added to the project portfolio list	Establishes project priorities and determines adjustments required to incorporate new projects onto the project portfolio list	Requests additional information during the review process Rejects proposed projects that are not aligned with strategic goals and objectives Provides business justification for projects rejected because of other reasons

✓ Project performance Index (monthly and cumulative)
✓ Critical issues needing resolution
3. **Completed projects**
   ✓ Final status (green, yellow, red)
   ✓ Cumulative performance index
   ✓ Benefits achieved and lessons learned
4. **Future projects:** anticipated to start in the next two months with mangers providing an overview of the project
   ✓ Project purpose, description, other departments being affected
   ✓ Preliminary milestone plan

The project portfolio management List is updated and minutes are published and distributed electronically within two days following the meeting.

PMCoE Logo

This chapter began with a reference to taking a journey and the importance of knowing the destination before beginning the trip. The concept of establishing formalized processes that help organize, plan, manage, and control the use of limited resources is critical to continued growth and in some cases the very survival of a company. Authorization is a foundation-building element that ensures alignment of projects with strategic goals and objectives. The institutionalization of project management occurs when the environment enables all of its employees to embrace its best practices as the normal way to do the work they do on a daily basis.

The integrity and stability of a four-legged stool depends on the strength of each leg as well as the connections (cross braces) between the legs. If one or more of the legs are weaker or shorter than the others, the integrity and stability of the stool is compromised and at risk of failure. The formation of a project management center of excellence is very similar to a four-legged stool with similar characteristics, each having four supporting elements (legs).

Figure 3–5. PMCoE Logo

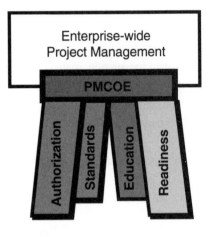

The integrity and stability of the PMCoE, like the stool, also requires equally strong and integrated supporting elements that are needed to facilitate the distribution of project management best practices enterprise-wide, as illustrated in Figure 3–5, the PMCoE logo, which is a stylized four-legged stool.

Summary

Effective distribution of corporate and business unit resources to manage projects is predicated on first establishing a formalized process to determine goals and objectives. This chapter discussed a method called Management by Planning that has proven to be very effective for one organization. Quantifying your capability and capacity to manage projects is a critical part of that process. Measuring project productivity and performance is a necessary part of determining your capability and capacity to complete projects on time and in budget. Instituting a project portfolio management process is a decisive requirement for successfully implementing project management best practices.

CHAPTER 4

Key Ingredients of a Methodology

Efficiency, proficiency, continuous improvement, and best in class are goals that in large part depend on a consistent application of procedures. These procedures, whose actions are guided by a regimen, are commonly referred to as *standards*. Standards are documented processes that, when universally adhered to, generally result in the successful achievement of goals. The importance of establishing and following standards is not always clearly understood by workers at all levels of an organization. However, the ability to achieve goals on a consistent basis lies in the unvarying adherence to the use of standards by everyone. There has been a shift in recent years in the area of nontechnical business processes away from standards documentation that describes the rules and procedures to be followed in infinite detail toward guidelines, which allow more flexibility in how they are applied and contain less detail. This is particularly true of project management methodologies. The trend in the past was to create multiple volumes of documentation describing project management procedures in excruciating detail with the thought that the standards would be used as training documents as well as standards to direct the management of projects. The only thing this approach to project management standards documentation did effectively was to gather dust.

The goal of the PMCoE is to establish modern project management knowledge and skills as a core competency requirement throughout the organization. Successful achievement of this aggressive goal requires a well-designed and implemented set of project management methodology guidelines.

Key Ingredients

The American Heritage Dictionary of the English Language defines *methodology* as "a body of practices, procedures, and rules used by those who work in a discipline."

Many of the project management methodologies attempt, but fail, to make strong connections to the Project Management Institute's (PMI®) Project Management Body of Knowledge (PMBOK®) Guide. These guidelines are universally recognized and accepted as the project management methodology standard, providing guiding principles for managing projects. This failure is due in part to a mistaken perspective, held by more than a few, that the PMBOK® Guide is itself a methodology for managing projects. The PMBOK® Guide is not a methodology, but a set of guidelines that identify specific practices, principles, techniques, and tools for managing projects of all sizes and types, regardless of industry. The difficulty companies encounter lies in their inability to translate the PMBOK® Guide into an effective methodology to help project managers and teams apply the PMBOK® Guide. The focus is typically on product development processes rather than project management processes to manage the work to make the deliverables required to create the products. These guidelines typically address critical milestones to develop new products with the emphasis on engineering requirements, customer requirements and industry and governmental regulations.

There is a misconception by some in the profession that the PMBOK® Guide needs to be expanded to become more relevant to various industries. There is common agreement that methodologies are needed to guide the development of products and services, and there is no argument that project management methodologies are necessary to ensure that new product development projects are properly managed. The simple answer lies in translating the PMBOK® Guide into a methodology that addresses the needs of the environment in which it will be used. The PMBOK® Guide is designed to be general in content, whereas a methodology is more industry specific since the application of project management practices is focused on the project or the industry where it is applied.

Generic Methodology

Section two of this book contains a sample generic project management methodology guideline (PMMG) that is based on the PMBOK® Guide five process groups. Each section of the PMMG contains one or more core processes including tools and templates. An education and training section is also included to identify the requisite knowledge and skills to enable an individual to effectively apply the PMMG core processes. A graphical representation of the various elements of the PMMG is shown in Figure 4–1.

Table 4–1 summarizes the table of contents for the PMMG. Each of the PMMG chapters contained in Section II (Chapters 8-13) are organized around the following paragraph headings:

- Section Overview
- Core Process Description
- Process Tools and Templates
- Process Flow Diagram
- Process Step Descriptions table
- RRAA Matrix table

The first PMMG section addresses processes that control the creation and management of the *portfolio of projects*. Sections 2 through 5 reflect the PMBOK® Guide core process groups that *identify, plan, coordinate, monitor,* and *end* projects in an orderly fashion. The last section contains an appraisal of core competency goals and lays out an education and training program to achieve those goals across the organization.

Figure 4–1. PMMG Diagram

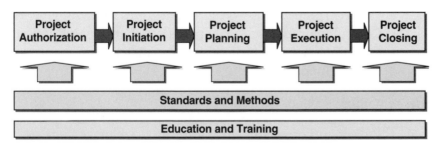

Table 4–1.   Methodology Contents

ID	PMMG Sections	Core Processes
1	Project Authorization	Annual project planning and capital budget development process
		Project request/authorization process
2	Project Initiation	Project initiation process
3	Project Planning	Project planning process
4	Project Execution	Project progress reporting cycle process
		Project issues resolution process
		Project change control process
5	Project Closing	Post project review process
		Metrics reporting process
6	Education and Training	Education and training goals
		Education and training requirements
		Education and training curriculum synopsis

An effective general purpose project management methodology guideline (PMMG) contains the following necessary ingredients, starting with an introduction that includes:

- Vision—inspiration it is trying to impart
- Purpose—how it will enable the organization
- Implementation—what it will enable
- Key definitions—clarification of common terms
- Methodology overview—layout of the contents
- Core process integration—initiation, planning, execution, control, and closing
- Process group definitions—initiation, planning, execution, control, and closing
- Project levels—scaling requirements of projects
- Project classifications—creating categories for requirements
- Controlling processes—key processes that vary by project
- Core process/classification matrix—match processes by classification

The remaining sections include:

- Project authorization—project portfolio management processes

- Project initiation—project start-up processes
- Project planning—project planning and readiness processes
- Project execution—status reporting and controlling processes
- Project closing—project wrap-up processes
- Education and training—knowledge and skills requirements
- Appendix—project tools and templates

Creating Classifications

A project management methodology should add value to the process of managing projects rather than simply providing administrative functions. It isn't practical or necessary to require all projects, regardless of size, complexity, duration, etc., to the use all 39 core and facilitating processes identified in the PMBOK® Guide. Use of project management processes should be scaled to fit the need for ensuring adequate controls are in place.

In some cases, it may make sense to modify certain process requirements and/or tools. For example, the scope statement or capital authorization request (CAR) may be adjusted for specific projects to ensure that requirements are scaled to add value and not unnecessary paperwork. These decisions should be made on a case-by-case basis. A classification system should establish guidelines to help define the minimum requirements for projects that meet different criteria and to ensure that the scaling of requirements is done on a consistent basis.

Table 4–2 shows a system created for an information technology center of excellence that classifies all projects into one of five levels based on three primary factors: project budget, project duration, and project boundaries. The first and third factors have more weight in determining classification than the project duration. These factors are used as general classification guidelines; however, other factors, such as the project's importance (strategic status) to the organization may influence a project's assignment to a higher classification level. The project classification matrix table

Table 4–2.   Project Classification Matrix

| | Project Classification Factors | | |
Level	Budget Amount	Duration (Months)	Boundaries
One	$0	0–3	Intradepartmental
Two	<$20K	<3	Intradepartmental
Three	$20–$100,000	3–6	IT cross-functional
Four	$100,000–$250,000	6–12	Interdepartmental
Five	>$250,000	>12	Global

illustrates how some simple factors can be used to determine the minimum requirements for projects in the five classifications.

Minimum Requirements for Early Implementers

Take small steps at the beginning and don't expect everyone to understand or appreciate the value of this new approach to managing projects. This is especially true if a formalized approach to managing projects is nonexistent. In this case, it is very important to focus on introducing minimum requirements at the start; otherwise efforts to get people to embrace the methodology will be viewed as unnecessary administrative tasks adding more management controls that increase an already overwhelming workload. We do not suggest that the methodology contents be reduced, but rather that initial requirements be limited until the PMCoE determines that the organization is ready to begin using more of the processes.

An article written by Tom Mochal entitled, "The Value of Project Management," discusses many of the same issues we have discussed in this and previous chapters. It also provides excellent rebuttals to those individuals who question the value of project management. Excerpts from the www.tenstep.com Web site are reprinted here with the permission of the author and the Web site.

Overcoming Resistance

Good project management discipline is the way to over-come many shortcomings. Having good project management skills does not mean you have no problems. It does not mean that risks go away. It does not mean that there are no surprises. The value of good project management is that you have standard processes in place to deal with all contingencies.

Project management processes and techniques are used to coordinate resources to achieve predictable results. However, it should be understood up front that project management is not totally a science, and there is never a guarantee of success. Because projects involve people, there is always complexity and uncertainty that cannot be absolutely controlled. So, project management is also partly an art that requires flexibility and creativity to be successful as well. It is a science because it relies on proven and repeatable processes and techniques to achieve project success. It is an art because it has a lot to do with managing and relating to people. Therefore the project manager also must rely on people management, good judgment, interpersonal skills, and personal intuition. A good project management methodology provides a framework, process, guidelines, and techniques to greatly increase the odds of being successful, and therefore provides value to the project and the project manager.

The value proposition for project management goes something like this. It takes time and effort to proactively manage a project. This cost is more than made up for over the life of the project by:

- Resolving problems more quickly
- Not working in areas that are outside of the scope of the project
- Resolving future risk before the problems occur
- Communicating and managing expectations with customers, team members, and stakeholders more effectively
- Building a higher quality product the first time

People who complain that project management is a lot of "overhead" forget the point. Your project is going to face issues. Do you want to proactively resolve them or figure them out as you go? Your project will face potential risks. Do you want to try to resolve them before they happen, or wait until the problems arise? Are you going to communicate proactively or deal with conflict caused by lack of project information? Are you going to manage scope or let scope manage you? Are you going to build quality into your process, or fix problems later when they will be more costly to resolve? The characteristics of the project are not going to change whether you use a formal project management process or not. What changes is how the events are dealt with when the project is in progress. Are they dealt with haphazardly and reactively? Or proactively with a smoothly running process?

After reading this, you might wonder why everyone does not utilize good project management techniques. Or you might think about yourself. Why aren't you using them? There are probably a couple reasons.

Good Project Management Requires an Upfront Investment of Time and Effort

Many people consider themselves to be "doers." They might not be as comfortable with their planning skills. Many times there is a tendency to discuss a problem, and then go out and fix it. This works when you have a five-hour change request. It doesn't work on a 5,000-hour project. Resist the urge to jump right in. The project will complete sooner if you properly plan it first, and then have the discipline to manage the project effectively.

Your Organization Is Not Committed

It's hard to be a good project manager in an organization that doesn't value project management skills. For instance, if you take the time to create a project definition document, and your client asks why you were wasting your time doing it, then probably you are not going to be very excited about the planning process on your next project. To be effective, the entire organization must be behind it.

You Don't Know How To

Sometimes it's not a matter of will, but a matter of skill. Sometimes people are asked to manage projects without the training or the experience necessary. In those cases, you struggle without the right tools or training to manage effectively.

You May Have Been Burned (or Buried) in the Past

A common criticism of methodology is that it is cumbersome, paper intensive, and takes too much focus away from the work at hand. Sometimes this criticism is a feature of the first bullet point. Other times, it is a legitimate concern caused by not scaling the methodology to the size of your project. For instance, if you were required to develop a fifteen-page project definition even if your project is only 250 hours, you may have been turned off. This is not usually a methodology problem as much as it is a misapplication of the methodology.

There Is a Fear of Control

Many people like to be able to solve problems and do their jobs creatively with a minimum of supervision. They might fear that formal project management techniques will result in tight controls that will take the fun out of the work. Common processes and procedures do eliminate some of the creativity in areas where you probably don't want it in the first place.

Although these may be reasons to be hesitant about using project management, they must be overcome. If you are new to this subject, you need to first understand the value proposition. If the result of project management were that projects would complete slower, cost more, and have poor quality, it would not make sense to use it. However, the opposite is true—using sound project management techniques and processes will give you a higher likelihood that your project will be completed on time, within budget, and to an acceptable level of quality.

That being said, when you use a project management process, be smart. Don't build the project management processes for a ten million dollar project if your project is only ten thousand dollars. Consider all aspects of how to manage a project, and build the right processes for your size project.

Four elements of project management knowledge areas are truly fundamental and critical to managing projects successfully. That is not to say the other five are less important, because they aren't; they just don't have the same degree of impact as the following four. They are development and maintenance of a:

- Scope statement
- Baseline schedule
- Communication plan
- Risk assessment

If an organization is taught to properly use these tools consistently and effectively the result will be more projects being completed successfully. Success is an enabler that reduces resistance from those who doubt the value that project management practices can provide to the organization, and it helps speed up the adoption of the other methodology processes.

Scope Statement   The scope statement identifies the project by name; provides an identification number; date and name of the preparer; customer representative; project sponsor; and project manager. It also identifies the project stakeholders, project team members, and steering team members (if one is required). It provides brief information on the corporate goals and objectives it supports, the purpose for the project, a description of what will be done, the anticipated business benefits and how they will be measured, and high-level requirements, specific inclusions and exclusions, project deliverables, constraints, assumptions, and critical success factors. A proposed project budget and project milestone plan along with spaces for customer representative, sponsor, project manager, and PMCoE approval signatures and dates are included. A scope statement change log table is added at the end of the document to record subsequent revisions.

Baseline Schedule   An effective project management baseline schedule contains a common organization structure that uses common summary level descriptions. These facilitate the ability to create a master schedule with all of the projects rolled up to the highest summary levels: initiation phase, planning phase, execution phase, and closing phase. Figure 4–2 shows the basic outline of a baseline schedule template.

Communication Plan   The communication plan is used to plan specific communication events that are repeated throughout the project life cycle, such as: project progress report meetings, steering team meetings, management review meetings, etc. The communication plan identifies the project by name, identification number, communication event, facilitator, purpose, timing/frequency, participants, location, and method of communication.

Risk Assessment   Risk assessment provides a means to document and rate project risk probability and impact and to establish priority ratings. The tool identifies the project by name, identification number, and date completed. The risks are numbered, briefly described, associated with a project task by description and schedule line number, determined to be an internal or external risk, and accompanied by a brief description of actions required and contingency plans (if the rating requires).

Figure 4–2. Baseline Schedule Template

1.0 Project name
    1.1 Project authorized start date
    1.2 Project initiation phase
        1.2.1 Project preparation
            1.2.1.1 Prepare scope statement
            1.2.1.2 Prepare baseline plan
            1.2.1.3 Establish reporting cycle
            1.2.1.4 Prepare communication plan
            1.2.1.5 Establish issue resolution procedures
            1.2.1.6 Establish change control procedures
            1.2.1.7 Establish project documents control
            1.2.1.8 Define project roles and responsibilities
            1.2.1.9 Develop risk management plan
            1.2.1.10 Develop project metrics plan
            1.2.1.11 Complete readiness review
        1.3 Project planning phase
        1.4 Project execution phase
        1.5 Project closing phase
        1.6 Project complete

Note: The tasks 1.0 through 1.2.1.11 are common to all project schedules, but the tasks listed below items 1.3 through 1.5 vary depending on the project.

It is strongly recommended that all tools and templates be standardized and used without modification. Modifications to standard templates must be restricted to a documented process, otherwise a proliferation of multiple variations will occur and the "standard" will no longer exist. Don't assume that the value of common processes is understood. In some organizations, there may be "pockets" where some level of project management practices are being followed, and they will have tools and templates that have been well accepted by most of the people in that unit. The strongest resistance to start using common tools and template formats comes from these areas. One of the best ways to remove resistance is to get those who have "ownership" of their templates involved in the process of creating the corporate standards.

    Appendix B contains examples of these four templates as well as all others associated with the PMMG. The templates are also on the CD-ROM included with this book.

Distributing a Project Management Methodology

The initial distribution of the methodology should be by a face-to-face presentation. Subsequent distributions of updates can be accomplished by placing the document file and associated templates on company LAN/WAN system in an area that is accessible to everyone. These should be read-only files. They could also be included on the PMCoE intranet Web site as downloadable files. In either case, the PMCoE secures the master copies of the methodology and associated templates for version control.

Face-to-face sessions require more time and planning than just making the documents available on the LAN/WAN or intranet. It is necessary to allow for a detailed review and discussion of the material, which is crucial to guaranteeing that the purpose and use is clearly understood. The business unit leader should distribute a personal communication to the organization stating that all department managers and those assigned to leading or managing projects are required to attend these sessions. The material can usually be covered in one two-hour session: the first hour is used to review and discuss the methodology document in detail; the second hour is used to review the proper use of the associated templates. The steps taken to prepare for the session are shown in Table 4–3.

Table 4–3.   PMMG Distribution Plan

Action	Responsible	Description of Action
Contact List	PMCoE	Contacts all department leaders and requests a list of their project leaders and project managers.
Purpose	PMCoE	Prepares and distributes a statement describing the session, including content, objectives, and anticipated learning outcomes. Publishes the announcement on the PMCoE intranet Web site (if one exists) in case others have an interest in participating.

continued

Table 4–3. *(Continued)*

Action	Responsible	Description of Action
Mandatory Attendance Announcement	Business Unit Leader	Issues a personal communication to the organization that all department leaders, project leaders, and project managers are required to attend a PMMG distribution session.
Registration Request	PMCoE	Prepares and distributes a session registration announcement two weeks before first date offered with multiple dates and times provided. Participants are asked to select their first, second, and third date/time slot choices. Limit time to respond to 24 hours.
Establish Session Lists	PMCoE	Summarizes the registrations, selects dates and times based on a group size limited to 6–8 people, which encourages more participation.
Registration Sign-up	Participants	Provides their name, department, position, phone number, and choices; first, second, and third.
Notification	PMCoE	Notifies participants of their assigned session date and time within 24 hours of registration closing so they can finalize their schedules and block out the time.
Plan For Changes	PMCoE	Anticipates changes to the list because they will occur. Plan on scheduling a catch-up session, but don't publicize it before the last class is completed.
Handouts	PMCoE	Prepares copies of the PMMG manual— including copies of all the associated templates—for each participant.
Reserve Facilities	PMCoE	Reserves the meeting room(s) at least two weeks in advance of the first meeting.
Hold Sessions	PMCoE	Holds sessions with great enthusiasm and have fun.
Recognition	PMCoE	Publishes a list of participants on the PMCoE intranet Web site and sends personal messages of appreciation to each participant.

Summary

Documenting formalized project management standards in the form of a methodology, common processes, tools, and templates is a prerequisite to distributing the disciplines and best practices of this important business function across the organization. Using basic characteristics to classify projects into several categories provides a way to "scale" requirements to fit the project where they add value rather than impose unnecessary controls. Initial distribution of the standards is best done in face-to-face sessions to ensure they are reviewed in detail and clearly understood. It also provides an opportunity to answer questions and give specific instructions in their proper use.

CHAPTER 5

Education and Training; Critical Success Factors

Providing basic training is the important next step after introducing the project management methodology guidelines (PMMG). Most organizations struggle and resist using the PMMG and the associated templates if some basic training in the fundamentals of project management is not provided immediately following the initial distribution of the standards. It does not make much sense to publish a methodology that represents a totally new concept to many of the users and expect them to willingly start using it on their own.

Completion of a project management fundamentals class should be a mandatory minimum requirement for all department managers, project managers, and team leaders. A project management fundamentals class should include:

- The history of project management as a profession
- Definitions of key word and terms
- Review of the PMBOK® Guide framework
- Overview of scope management processes and templates
- Overview of time management processes and templates
- Overview of communication management processes and templates
- Overview of risk management processes and templates
- Introduction to use of scheduling software (MS Project 98/2000)

Basic training with this content delivered with both lecture and hands-on exercises can be covered comfortably in one two-day session or four half-day sessions. The planning process outlined in

Chapter 4 for the initial distribution of the PMMG is an excellent process to follow when planning and scheduling basic training classes.

The Importance of Education and Training

A comprehensive project management education and training program is necessary to meet the needs of the organization's general population, project team members, project managers, and management staff at all levels.

If modern project management knowledge, skills, tools, and techniques are not being commonly applied in the management of projects, resulting in projects that are not meeting customer's expectations for cost, time, and quality, a strong case can be made for formal education and training.

Education and training to learn special skills are generally included in the annual budget in most companies, especially in the areas that require technical knowledge to do the job. Yet management in many organizations is reluctant to earmark funds specifically for project management training. There is a general expectation that untrained and inexperienced employees assigned to manage projects will be able to meet time and cost objectives on a consistent basis because they are often subject matter experts in a technical area, such as engineering or information technology. Formal education and training, however, are critical success factors in the consistent completion of projects that exceed customers' expectations.

Elements of an Education and Training Program

A comprehensive project management education and training program is based on establishing the following requirements:

- Business objectives
- Performance objectives
- Competencies

- Knowledge
- Skills
- Attitude

Table 5–1 shows the education and training format used to document the requirements of the education and training program.

Section II, Chapter 14 contains an example of a comprehensive education and training program that addresses the needs of an organization's general population, team members, project managers, executives, and managers in three areas: knowledge objectives, learning objectives, and assessment methods. The program also identifies the level of learning required of each audience, and validates the effectiveness of the education and training in each area for the four primary audience groups.

Table 5–1. Education and Training Goals Requirements

Goals	General Population	Team Members	Project Managers	Functional Managers
Business Objectives	Support the goal to establish project management as a core competency and achieve a world-class proficiency.	Support the goal to establish project management as a core competency.	Manage projects that are completed on time and within budget and meet or exceed customer expectations.	Improve project success and productivity. Achieve corporate strategic planning goals and objectives through effective project management practice.
Performance Objectives	Conversant awareness of the methodology as the project management standard.	Consistent application of project management processes as documented in the methodology.	Consistent use of the methodology to manage projects.	Proactive support of the use of methodology on all projects.

continued

Table 5–1. *(Continued)*

Goals	General Population	Team Members	Project Managers	Functional Managers
Competencies	Have conversant knowledge of the principles and practices of project management.	Demonstrate effective application of project management processes as contained in methodology.	Demonstrate effective application of the methodology processes to complete projects on time and within budget.	Establish prioritized department project portfolio and effectively utilize the methodology to manage the work.
Knowledge	Familiarity with project management terms and acronyms.	Working knowledge of project management processes as contained in the methodology.	Working knowledge of project management processes as contained in the methodology.	Working knowledge of project management processes as contained in the methodology.
Skill	Demonstrate a basic understanding of the project management processes.	Demonstrated ability to effectively apply project management processes contained within the methodology.	Demonstrated ability to effectively apply and lead others in the application of project management processes contained within the methodology.	Demonstrated ability to effectively support and enforce the application of project management processes contained within the methodology.
Attitude	Accept management's goal to establish project management practices as a core competency across the organization.	Show a desire to effectively apply project management practices at a core competency level.	Show a desire to effectively apply project management practices at a core competency level.	Support and encourage the adoption of project management as core competency organization goal.

The Internal Project Management Certification Program

In 1984 the Project Management Institute (PMI®) began a certification program for certifying project managers with the designation of Project Management Professional (PMP®). This certification is recognized by organizations worldwide as a respected credential, the first such program of its kind to achieved ISO-9000 certification. An increasing number of organizations use the PMP® as a baseline requirement for assigning or hiring project managers to manage projects of any significance. Many of these same companies have also developed their own internal qualification and certification programs for developing project management knowledge and skills. The knowledge and experience required to obtain PMP® certification is not specific to any one industry, but rather focuses on the application of processes, tools, and techniques contained in the PMBOK® Guide. Therefore, internal programs typically include PMP® certification as well as additional industry-specific training in the application of project management practices.

Internal qualification and certification programs are typically developed as a means to establish a project management career path within the organization. It is through this career path that the organization develops its own project management professionals for the future. Establishing the project management career path provides many benefits; for example, it

- Influences retention of valuable employees
- Convinces new job candidates to join the company
- Increases management skills enterprise-wide
- Motivates continuous improvement actions
- Improves project performance at all levels

The first step in this career path is qualification, which designates the individual has successfully demonstrated he or she has met the knowledge requirements of that level. Certification is achieved by demonstrating proficiency in applying the knowledge and skill learned at that level on one or more projects. Certification is

Table 5–2. Certification Requirements

Program Step	Project Classification	Time
Entry	Levels one and two	6 months
Intermediate	Levels three and four	1 year
Advanced	Level five	2 years

required at each level prior to advancing to the next step in the program. Table 5–2 shows the correlation between program certification and project classification, which is defined in the project classification matrix table shown in Chapter 4, Table 4–2.

Developing the Education and Training Program

Developing a project management education and training program is approached much like you would any other subject matter. There is a plethora of companies in the market place whose business is providing project management education and training. Most of them offer to customize their offerings to meet your specific needs. Most consultants want to sell you a package rather than spend the time to first understand what you really need. This is understandable because time is money and most companies are reluctant to pay outside consultants to develop customized education and training programs.

Performing the surveys and assessments presented in Chapter 2 provides valuable information to establish the baseline of current knowledge and skills. Bringing in outside consultants to perform the surveys and assessments typically produces more accurate and usable information. The other option is to use the tools presented in Chapter 2, or something similar. Analyzing the gap between the baseline and goal requirements provides the details needed to develop an effective curriculum. This requires a significant amount of knowledge and experience that is seldom found in-house. Thus this is one area where hiring outside consultants can produce better re-

Figure 5–1. Project Management Education and Training
Delivery Consortium

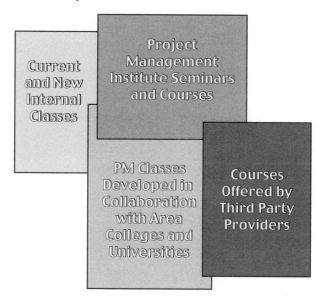

sults faster and in the long run cheaper than trying to do it in-house. The key to getting the best return on your investment when using outside consultants is to clearly define your requirements and expectations for them, work with them to develop a detailed plan for each step of the process, and review their progress on a regular basis. In other words, apply good project management practices throughout the project life cycle.

Figure 5–1 shows another approach that some organizations have used to provide excellent results.

Summary

Education and training are cornerstones of the foundation that supports the successful adoption of project management best practices. It will surely fail if management does not support the development and implementation, both financially and practically, by their participation. Finding skilled and experienced project managers in the job market today is very difficult, especially those who are PMP® certified. Retention and "growing your own" is the key to meeting your current and future needs, because their availability on the open market will increase slowly while the demand will continue to grow faster as more and more organizations adopt project management as a core business function.

CHAPTER 6

Ready-Set-Go!

L ast but not least, the fourth element of the PMCoE supporting structure is readiness. Determining readiness is the last thing done just before work on the project begins to complete deliverables. Evaluating readiness also occurs on strategic projects between project phases and at the end of the project (see Figure 6–1). Performing readiness checks is similar to checking the car over before you start off on a long trip; it doesn't keep bad things from happening, but it does provide some comfort and reduces the risk of things going wrong. Readiness checks are needed the most in the early stages of implementing the methodology. Once the organization's project management capability has matured, say to level three (more about this in Chapter 7), the initial readiness check by the PMCoE could be reduced to periodic reviews as deemed necessary.

It usually takes a while for organizations to become acclimated to new business processes and comfortable to the point that some degree of proficiency is attained. Experience has shown that implementing a project management methodology usually encounters some degree of resistance from project managers who feel concerned they might not "get it right" the first time or they just want to "get on with it," believing readiness checks are an unnecessary waste of time. Some executives and department managers may also believe this process isn't needed and just slows the project down. A good way to counteract these forms of resistance is to point out that readiness checks are not performed to evaluate performance—there are no good or bad grades assigned. They are done to help the project team ensure that it is properly prepared to achieve success before work begins, which saves time and money in the end.

Figure 6–1.   Project Review Process

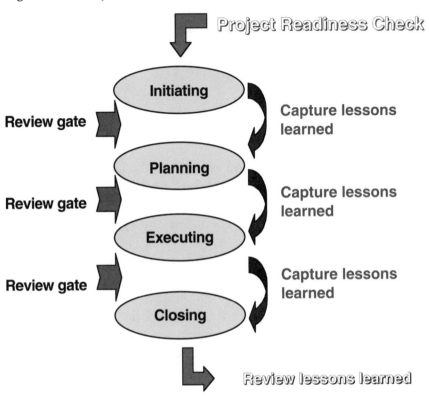

Performing a Readiness Review

It is preferable that the full project team, project customer representative, and project sponsor be present and participate in the readiness check. Having the customer and sponsor attend the readiness review communicates the importance of being prepared to everyone. The review process also provides another opportunity to validate that customer requirements and expectations have been communicated and are clearly understood by the project team. The process is shown in Figure 6–2 and explained in Table 6–1.

Table 6–2 is an abbreviated sample of the readiness review form that is signed by the project customer representative, project sponsor, project manager, and PMCoE representative to authorize

Figure 6–2. Readiness Review Process

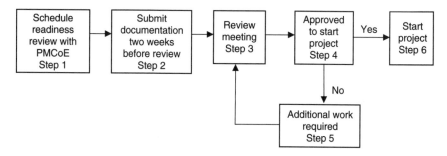

the project to proceed. A complete version of the form is included in Appendix B as PMMG template 1.10.

Additional project reviews are held between project phases on larger strategic projects. The customers' representative, project sponsor, project manager and team members, and the PMCoE

Table 6–1. Readiness Review Process Description

Step	Responsibility	Action Taken
1. Schedule	Project Manager	Contacts PMCoE 3-4 weeks before meeting date to schedule the review.
2. Documentation	Project Manager	Submits copies of all the required process documents to the PMCoE a minimum of two weeks before the meeting.
3. Meeting	PMCoE	Chairs the meeting where the project manager and team members present the process documents and describe how they will be used. The customer representative and sponsor can ask questions at this time as needed.
4. Decision	PMCoE, Customer, Sponsor	A decision is made if additional information or work is required on the documentation.
5. Not Approved	Project Manager	If additional information or work is required, the project manager will indicate a date when the team will be ready for another review.
6. Approved	PMCoE	Signs the review form and work on the project can proceed.

Table 6–2. Readiness Review Checklist

Project ID:	Project Name:				Level

Scheduled Review Date:

Req'd	PMMG Template	Are the following documents completed and/or process in place?	Completed YES	NO	Comments
	PMMG A	Project status update cycle established			
	PMMG B	Change control process established			
	PMMG C	Issues resolution process established			
	PMMG D	Steering team identified and in place			
	PMMG 1.7	Approved baseline plan			
	PMMG 1.8	Approved project budget			
	PMMG 1.9	Approved scope statement			
	PMMG 2.7	Team RRAA matrix completed			
	PMMG 2.8	Communication plan completed			
	PMMG 2.9	Risk assessment completed			
	PMMG 2.11	Metrics plan completed			
	PMMG 2.12	Configuration management plan completed			
		Capital funds request approved			

Review sign-off required:

Project Customer:	Project Sponsor:	Project Manager:	PMCoE	Approved to Proceed:	
				Yes	No
Date:	Date:	Date:	Date:		

representative are involved in these reviews as well. The purpose of gate reviews is to have the project team present the current status of the project, report on deliverables made to date (if any), and establish that the project is on track to achieves its objectives and goals as stated at the start. This review also identifies what work and deliverables will be accomplished during the next phase of the project.

Post Project Reviews

Post project reviews are critical to the continued improvement and growth of project management practices within any organization.

Unfortunately they do not occur as often as they should, with "not enough time" or "the next project is already started" the common excuse. Post project review meetings are as critical as readiness reviews before the project begins. Establishing project management best practices cannot be done without incorporating lessons learned to improve the methodology, processes, procedures, tools, and templates. These improvements will not be identified if a formal process isn't followed to ensure they are documented. Continuous improvement programs are based on formal reviews. Whether the project is deemed to have been a success or not, the post project review can provide all the project participants an opportunity to learn from what worked well and what did not. The next project will be better for it. See Appendix B for an example of the PMMG 4-2 Post Project Review Report.

Summary

The saying goes "We never have time to do it right the first time, but always have time to do it over." Project readiness reviews make sure the team will get it right the first time, and that it stays on track. In some cases, the project is canceled before it consumes too many wasted resources if that is determined to be the best choice. Effective project management begins and ends with processes that ensure continued improvement and growth. Without them the organization will take longer to mature.

CHAPTER 7

Maturity Takes Time

The American Heritage Dictionary of the English Language defines maturity as *"having reached full natural growth or development; having reached a desired or final condition of, relating to, or characteristic of full development, either mental or physical."* Based on this definition, it is safe to say that organizations have the ability to mature in terms of their knowledge, skills, and capability as time progresses. In the process of maturing, organizations and individuals either gain or lose ground, but they never stand still. Determining the level of project management maturity is a topic that has created a great deal of interest in the business world in recent years. A number of project management maturity models have been presented in various publications by both organizations and individuals since the mid 1990s, which have created an increased level of interest in the development of a standard. So much so that in 1997 the PMI® Standards Committee created the "Organization Project Management Maturity Model" (OPM3®) project. The objective is to develop a model that is intended to become a standard for measuring the project management maturity of an organization. The project team presented the initial draft of this model at the PMI® 2001 Annual Symposium Standards Committee in Nashville, Tennessee on November 4, 2001.

One of the reasons there is so much interest in establishing a project management maturity model standard is that some organizations want to be able to measure their capabilities of applying project management best practices against others in a particular industry, and against their competitors in particular, to see how they measure up. Another reason, which probably is more prevalent, is to use the model to help identify the steps required to achieve improvement and measure their progress toward accomplishing the highest level of performance in the model. Most of the maturity models share common elements, especially at the highest level—continuous improvement as an enterprise-wide capability.

The important lesson to learn about using models is that regardless of the one being followed, models need to be modified to fit the organization that uses them. No two companies apply project management the same way, because the products and environments differ from one company to another. Let's compare project management with finance, for example. Every company follows the standard practices and principles of finance established by the profession. However, they each apply them differently because their application is influenced by many different variables, such as the size of the business, the type of products or services, the number of accounts, industry/governmental rules and regulations, the use of manual versus computerized financial systems, etc. Project management as a business function also follows standard practices and principles established by its profession, and they also are applied differently in every company because of the same or similar influences.

Part of the maturing process is that organizations must ask the question; "What must we do to effectively implement enterprise-wide project management?" We have heard this question posed by a large majority of the 200-plus companies that attended the two-day seminar entitled: "Project Support Office: A Format for Development," in 1997 and 1998. Some of these companies have well-established localized project offices, but are hitting a wall of resistance that limits their penetration across the organization. The answer lies in establishing the supporting elements of authorization, standards, education, and readiness, as well as closing the gap among the four areas of influence found in every organization. These four areas are the management of projects, management of products, management of environment, and management of organizational change. The means to accomplish the realignment and closure of gaps are found in a concept called managing organizations by projects (MOBP), which was introduced in recent years by Paul C. Dinsmore. He refers to it as a holistic way of applying classic project management methodology on an enterprise-wide scale. Dinsmore's book *Winning in Business with Enterprise*

Figure 7–1. Management of Projects

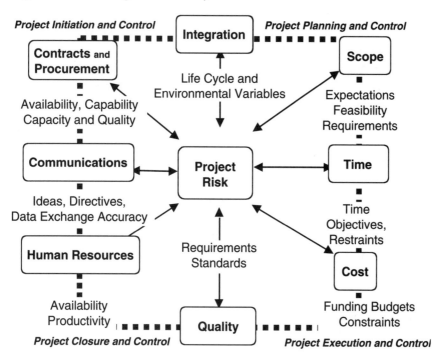

Project Management is a must read for those who want to succeed in establishing enterprise-wide project management. MOBP is a new philosophical point of view of how work should be done in a project-based organization. MOBP is a strategy, not a process. MOBP is the adoption of project management disciplines and practices as a methodology for completing almost all forms of work performed in an organization. MOBP is an integral part of the maturing processes that organizations typically go through to achieve the highest level of excellence. The four key areas of influence are shown in Figure 7–1, Figure 7–2, Figure 7–3, and Figure 7–4.

Effectively incorporating project management to manage the work performed for projects requires that product management processes be changed. The integration of product management and project management processes typically causes some degree of resistance at various levels of the organization. This unfamiliarity

Paul C. Dinsmore, *Winning in Business with Enterprise Project Management* (New York: AMACOM, 1999)

causes some people to question the value of project management and the need to make changes in the way they do their work or the way it is being managed. This level of resistance will diminish as the MOBP strategy is understood and accepted.

The management of products involves six key elements, as shown in Figure 7–2. These elements directly impact how effectively project management processes are inculcated into the culture of the organization. The product management elements exist to some degree in every organization, but they are often not formally recognized and documented. If project management is to become more than a systemic approach to managing single projects involving products and services, these product management elements must be clearly defined and formally documented, and project management processes must be an integral aspect.

The management of environment contains eight key components as shown in Figure 7–3. They affect project management

Figure 7–2.   Management of Products

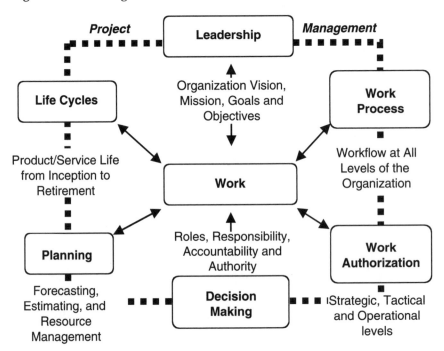

Figure 7–3. Management of Environment

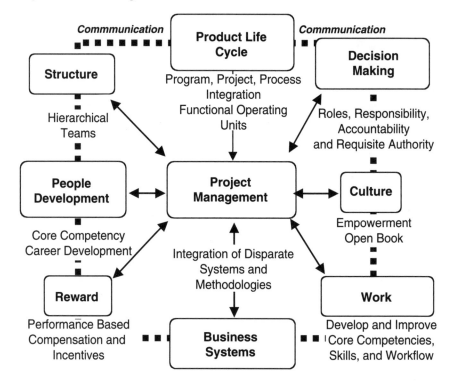

processes as they interface with the product management processes that guide the development of products and services. These environmental components are often missing or incomplete and seldom formally documented in organizations struggling to implement effective project management. The greatest number of disconnects and misalignments are usually found between the management of projects and the management of products. Both are heavily influenced by the eight components contained within the management of environment. These disconnects produce the greatest impediment to an effective implementation of project management in most organizations.

The most significant changes are typically required in the environmental components. They impact everyone in the organization at all levels. These changes therefore present the greatest challenges for managing change, as shown in Figure 7–4.

Figure 7–4.   Management of Organizational Change

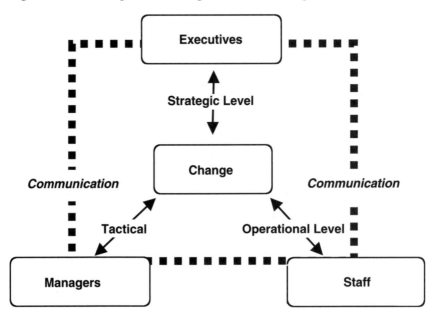

Whenever changes of the magnitude discussed in this book are introduced, some level of resistance occurs at all three functional levels of the organization. Whenever changes affecting someone's area of responsibility are implemented, there is a natural tendency to resist that change. The first step in managing change is to recognize that resistance is a natural response. Most resistance can be effectively reduced or eliminated with frequent clear communications and by directly involving those who are affected most in the process of developing and implementing the change. Personal involvement provides an opportunity to affect how the change is implemented and thereby to take some ownership of the change.

All four areas of influence—management of projects, management of products, management of environment, and management of organizational change—must be assessed to establish the current status of each component. The company should ultimately be assessed as a whole, but the initial assessment process typically involves only one segment of the company at a time. Assessments are best managed by targeting one functional unit where the majority of projects occur, such as information technology or engineering. Limiting the boundaries of the assessment reduces the cost and time required to conduct the assessment, while at the same time provides a good reading of the current status in each of the four areas of influence. It is best to select the portion of the organization (division, business unit, department, or group) that has adopted some level of project management and is effective to some degree in its application. This provides a friendly and more manageable environment in which to perform the initial assessment. The initial assessment results provide a baseline, identifying both best and worst practices, for measuring the unit's own progress in making improvements as well as a basis for measuring the remainder of the organization as it is assessed in comparison to its own best practices.

Stages of Maturity

Once the decision has been made to establish the PMCoE as a business function, there is often a significant amount of pressure on the PMCoE to move quickly to show significant benefits that support the decision by upper management. The speed at which the PMCoE is able to move depends largely on the degree of executive support that is behind the effort and the level of commitment they give at the start in the form of dedicated resources (budget and staff). The time it takes to show positive progress and demonstrate improvements also depends on the initial project management maturity level of the organization. This level may require adding project management professionals from outside the organization as permanent or temporary staff if the required talent is not available inside to complete the work required. The PMCoE leadership must respond to this pressure by reminding the executive team of the ultimate goal, which is to distribute an integrated project management strategy across the organization. This is a significant undertaking and it takes time to accomplish because progress can only move as fast as the organization's ability to adopt these new concepts. Figure 7–5 depicts the PMCoE's

Figure 7–5. PMCoE Organization Maturity

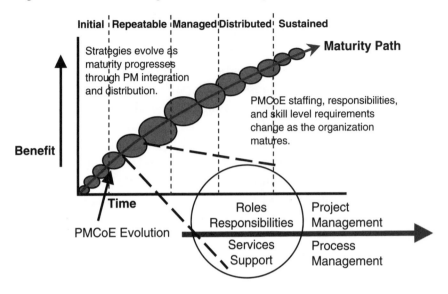

maturity path with a corresponding evolution of its roles and responsibilities as the organization matures.

The PMCoE begins as a small organization focused on establishing its presence within each level of the company. The initial objective is to create and distribute a standard methodology. This is followed by providing basic training in the fundamentals of project management at all levels. The pace of this stage of maturity depends to a large degree on the level of commitment and support given by the executive management team and level of resistance the PMCoE receives across the organization. The most effective method for rolling out the PMCoE structure is to establish it first at the corporate level, then set it up next in only one business unit where the most support for implementing project management best practices exists. Demonstrating success and improvements early in the implementation stage generates more support across the organization and helps convince those who may be questioning the cost versus the value it adds to the company.

Figure 7–5 shows a PMCoE maturity path that can occur if the maturity model shown in Figure 7–6 is followed.

Figure 7–6. PMCoE Maturity Model

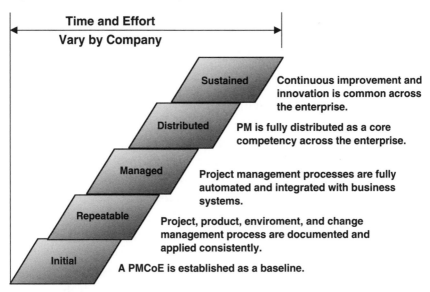

The PMCoE structure evolves over time as the organization's project management maturity increases. The PMCoE scope is narrow at the beginning, typically being limited to one level of the company, and is focused on establishing the basic building blocks to create standards, tools, and templates as well as to provide basic training. Its role expands as the organization structure moves into all areas of the company. It takes on a more active mentoring and coaching role with expanded education and training offered as well. Implementation of automated systems and integration with other business systems typically require added staff for a period of time. As the organization passes the third stage, "managed" staffing sizes can usually be reduced and the scope changes to focus more on forecasting and future planning activities, because the need for personal coaching and mentoring has been greatly reduced by the organization's advanced maturity. Figure 7–6 shows a PMCoE maturity model. A number of project management maturity models are available in the market in addition to the Organization Project Management Maturity Model (OPM3)® currently being developed by PMI®.

The amount of time it takes an organization to achieve full maturity, "sustained" fifth stage, can vary significantly from one company to another. It is doubtful that any organization has yet reached the last stage of maturity at this point. However, many organizations have achieved the third stage and parts of the "distributed" fourth stage and are continuing toward the highest level of maturity. Table 7–1 provides a brief list of defining characteristics that should be observable in the organization at each level.

The capabilities described as characteristics in Table 7–1 are provided as examples only to expand on the model shown in Figure 7–1. It is not unusual for an organization to exhibit some of the characteristics in more than one stage. However, moving from one stage of the maturity model to the next higher level requires that all of the characteristics be met on a consistent basis. It is not possible to skip a stage, say from stage one *Initial* to stage three *Managed,* because the organization is going through a maturing process that requires time. It is the consistent application of all the characteristics across the enterprise that determines the completion of a stage. It should be fairly obvious by now why establishing project management as a core competency enterprise-wide is a worthy goal, and a most difficult and nontrivial undertaking.

Benchmarking

Benchmarking, both internal and external, is an essential activity to pursue in the maturing process. Learning from others by leveraging their experiences to increase your own knowledge and skills is the fastest, most effective way to grow. Creating the PM knowledge network, which serves the purpose of an internal network is an important step. One of the primary benefits the PM knowledge network provides is the opportunity to benchmark the project management maturity of other departments and business units. Internal benchmarking is the most effective way to establish best practices enterprise-wide.

External benchmarking is another important part of improving the organization's project management maturity. One of the

Table 7–1. Maturity Characteristics

Stage	Characteristics
Initial	• No formal methodology in place for managing projects. • Projects are managed adhoc and success is not repeatable. • No formal training and education program exists. • Projects are typically late and over budget if completed at all. • No project review process exists. • No master list of projects exists. • No project authorization process exists. • Project risk assessment is nonexistent.
Repeatable	• PMCoE structure is established at some levels. • A standard methodology is created and distributed. • Project management fundaments are provided at all levels. • Project portfolio management has been implemented. • Management monthly reviews projects. • 25–50% of project deliveries are on time and within budget.
Managed	• PMCoE structure is established enterprise-wide. • PMMG is automated and integrated with other business systems. • PM qualification/certification program is in place. • Internal intranet is used extensively for all PM functions. • Virtual and real-time project status reporting is common. • 50–75% of project deliveries are on-time and within budget. • PM education and training is a requirement at all levels.
Distributed	• PM lessons learned knowledge database is in place. • PMP® certification is required of all project managers. • All employees require basic PM knowledge and skills as a minimum core capability for their jobs. • 75–95% of project deliveries are on time and within budget.
Sustained	• Management by projects is a company philosophy. • Executives and managers are PMP® certified. • All project managers must complete internal qualification/certification program. • Continuous improvements are commonplace in all areas. • 99% of project deliveries are on time and within budget.

best project management benchmarking opportunities is offered by an organization called Human Systems Knowledge Network, Inc. (http://www.hskni.com or contact Dalton Weekly, at dweekley@hskni. com) based out of Seattle, Washington. Dalton Weekley's organization serves as the U.S. representative of

Human Systems Limited (http://www.humansystems.co.uk or mailto: info@humansystems.co.uk), an organization based in the United Kingdom. Human Systems is the world's leading provider of project management benchmarking networks. The following information, extracted from its Web site, explains the importance of benchmarking.

> Benchmarking is a discipline that has developed during the past twenty years or so as a means of searching for the practices that lead to superior performance, and of measuring the performance of comparable processes in different companies, and even in different industries. It has given rise to expressions that are now common currency in management—expressions such as "best practice," "best in class," and "world class." In order to apply the technique to project management, three challenges in particular have needed to be overcome.

Uniqueness of Projects

Benchmarking is a discipline that was developed in the context of processes, so it is important to understand how projects differ from processes. Every project is to some extent unique—that is a major element in most definitions of what a project is. Thus, although project management utilizes repetitive processes, there is more to projects than the sum of the processes involved.

Differing Project Environments

Project teams undertake projects, but before they can be undertaken they need to be defined and initiated. This process of project definition takes place within a specific context that depends on the industry, the specific enterprise(s) undertaking the project, and the functional disciplines involved in the project.

Developing Trust

Trust and mutual cooperation are essential characteristics of the data-gathering stages of all effective benchmarking exercises, but this is particularly true for projects. The uniqueness of each individual project, and the different corporate and industry environments within which projects take place, encourage the facile dismissal of externally gathered data as "not relevant."

Summary

Establishing project management as a core discipline across the organization is an arduous task that requires patience and steadfastness. Those who persevere in their efforts will be rewarded by the many benefits that come as the organization moves up the maturity ladder. The time and effort required to reach the top varies from company to company, but the rewards are similar in every case; recognition by customers and industry peers alike as world-class providers of products and services in their field.

Section II of the book follows this chapter. It contains a complete, unabridged version of the generic Project Management Methodology Guidelines developed to provide a model for organizations that are just beginning to establish a formal project management discipline. This model, along with the tools and templates contained in Appendix B are also contained on the enclosed CD-ROM found inside the back cover of the book. The PMMG document and associated tools can be easily modified to suit any organization's specific needs.

SECTION II

✛

Project Management Methodology Guidelines

CHAPTER 8

Introduction to a Methodology

Vision

The vision of the Project Management Center of Excellence (PMCoE) organization is to achieve a world-class proficiency in the consistent application of project management practices, processes, procedures, tools, and techniques. The goal is to inculcate project management as a core capability discipline that is part of the fabric of the work that is performed. Achieving world-class status results in *consistently* exceeding customer expectations for the products and services that it provides.

Purpose

The Project Management Institute's (PMI®) Project Management Body of Knowledge (PMBOK®) Guide is universally recognized and accepted as the project management methodology standard and provides the guiding principles on which this methodology is based. These modern project management practices have been adapted to create a unique methodology to guide the global management of projects in a consistent and reliable manner. This methodology is referred to as the Project Management Methodology Guidelines (PMMG). The PMMG provides a blueprint for planning a project or program and its sub-projects; monitoring schedule, scope, and resource information; controlling the project schedule, scope, and resources based on information collected; and reporting on progress. In the remaining sections of this document, the PMMG identifies core processes to be followed to complete the work during various phases. The PMMG is a contiguous framework of processes, each relying on the proper application of the others, while at the same time it is a set of separate, definable processes that can stand alone. These processes can and should be scaled to suit the requirements of the designated project classifications or functional elements of a total program.

Implementation

Development, distribution, implementation, and maintenance of the PMMG are the responsibility of the Project Management Center of Excellence (PMCoE). The PMCoE is also chartered to support and assist project teams through coaching and mentoring, in the proper application of project management practices, to enable consistent successful completion of projects. We hope that these guidelines will facilitate the rapid deployment of modern project management practices in the form of common processes that will be applied in all areas of the organization. Enterprise-wide acceptance and adoption of the PMMG as a standard will help establish a mature environment that enhances the capability for continuous improvement through effective applications of lessons learned.

Methodology Overview

The PMMG is composed of five process groups. Each contains one or more core processes using standard tools and templates. An education and training section is also included to identify the requisite knowledge and skills to enable an individual to effectively apply the PMMG core processes. A graphical representation of the various elements of the PMMG is shown in Figure 8–1.

The Project Management Methodology Guidelines (PMMG) map shown in Table 8–1 provides a summarized table of contents for the PMMG. The first PMMG section addresses processes that control the creation and management of the portfolio of projects. Sections 2 through 5 reflect the PMI® PMBOK® Guide core process

Figure 8–1. PMMG Diagram

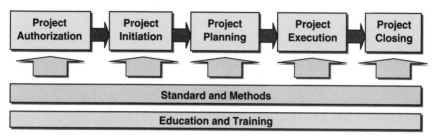

groups that *identify, plan, coordinate, monitor,* and *end* projects in an orderly fashion. The last section contains core processes that assess current project management knowledge and skills, establishes core competency goals, and lays out an education and training program to achieve those goals across the organization.

Core Process Integration

Because projects are unique undertakings, they involve a degree of uncertainty. Organizations performing projects usually divide each project into several *project phases* to provide better management

Table 8–1. Methodology Map

ID	PMMG Sections	Core Processes
1	Project Authorization	Annual project planning and capital budget development process project request/ authorization process
2	Project Initiation	Project initiation process
3	Project Planning	Project planning process
4	Project Execution	Project progress reporting cycle process
		Project issues resolution process
		Project change control process
5	Project Closing	Post project review process
		Metrics reporting process
6	Education and Training	Education and training goals
		Education and training requirements
		Education and training curriculum synopsis

control. Collectively, the project phases are known as the *project life cycle*.

Project Phase Definitions

The following provides a brief definition of each of the five project phases that are an integral part of the PMMG.

Initiating Phase   Obtaining formal approval for the project; the project charter is issued.

Planning Phase   Determining the project requirements, customer expectations, objectives, and benefits and creating the project baseline plan.

Executing Phase   The work is done according to the plan to meet deliverable requirements. Status is tracked and reported. Scope control is carefully monitored in this phase of the project.

Controlling Processes   Processes are established to identify and resolve issues, and manage changes that affect project, cost, timing, and quality. A process to measure and record project metrics is also established and implemented in the executing phase of the project.

Closing Phase   Contracts are closed and final customer approval is obtained for the end deliverable. Post project evaluations are reviewed and lessons learned are documented.

Project Levels

A project management methodology should add value to the process of managing projects rather than simply providing administrative functions. Therefore, the determination of which project management processes are required should be scaled to fit projects of varying classifications. In some cases, it makes sense to modify certain process requirements and/or tools, such as the scope statement or capital authorization request (CAR), to ensure that the requirements add value and not unnecessary paperwork. These decisions should be made on a case-by-case basis. The following classification structure has been established to help define the minimum requirements for projects that meet different criteria.

All projects are classified into one of five levels by considering three primary factors: project budget, project duration, and project boundaries. The first and third factors have more weight in determining classification than the project duration. These factors are used as general classification guidelines, however other factors such as the project's importance (strategic status) to the organization may influence a project's assignment to a higher classification level in some cases. The Project Classification Matrix (see Table 8–2) provides a quick reference to determine the minimum requirements for projects in the five classifications.

Note the Core Process Templates—Classification Matrix (Table 8–4) is organized in the order in which each component is used on a typical project.

The controlling processes identified in Table 8–3 are critical to the successful completion to every project classified as level three through five.

Table 8–2. Project Classification Matrix

	Project Classification Factors		
Level	Budget Amount	Duration (Months)	Boundaries
One	$0	0–3	Intradepartmental
Two	<$20,000	<3	Intradepartmental
Three	$20,000–$100,000	3–6	IT cross-functional
Four	$100,000–$250,000	6–12	Interdepartmental
Five	>$250,000	>12	Global

Table 8–3. Controlling Processes

(X = Required, O = Optional)

Process ID	Process Tools Name	L 1	L 2	L 3	L 4	L 5
A	Project Status Reporting Cycle		X	X	X	X
B	Change Control Process		O	X	X	X
C	Issues Resolution Process		O	X	X	X
D	Steering Team Roles		O	X	X	X

Table 8–4 provides an association between the processes and templates found in the remainder of this document with the classification table shown above.

Figure 8–2 and Tables 8–5 and Table 8–6 show the process followed by a level 1 project. Level 1 projects are small projects requiring much less effort to manage than projects in level 2 through 5. The processes for managing level 2 through 5 projects are found in the following chapters.

Table 8–4. Core Process Templates

(X = Required, O = Optional)

ID	Template Name	L 1	L 2	L 3	L 4	L 5
Project Initiation						
1.0	Project Profile		O	X	X	X
1.1	Project Selection		O	X	X	X
1.2	Project Charter		O	X	X	X
1.3	Potential Impact		O	X	X	X
1.4	Preliminary Communication Plan		O	X	X	X
1.5	Small Project Summary	X				
1.6	Project Summary (See Request/ Authorization Process)		X	X	X	X
1.7	Project Plan (Initiate at milestone level; expand to baseline)		X	X	X	X

continued

Table 8–4. *(Continued)*

(X = Required, O = Optional)

ID	Template Name	L 1	L 2	L 3	L 4	L 5
1.8	Budget Worksheet		O	X	X	X
1.9	Scope Statement		X	X	X	X
1.10	Readiness Checklist		O	X	X	X
1.11	Project Portfolio Management Report		O	X	X	X
Project Planning						
2.1	Process Analysis		O	X	X	X
2.2	Voice of the Customer		O	X	X	X
2.3	Critical to Quality		O	X	X	X
2.4	Business Requirements		O	X	X	X
2.5	Alternate Solutions		O	O	O	O
2.6	Records Administration		X	X	X	X
2.7	RRAA Matrix (Roles, Responsibilities, Accountability, Authority)		O	X	X	X
2.8	Communication Plan		O	X	X	X
2.9	Risk Assessment		O	O	X	X
2.10	Skills Matrix		O	O	O	O
2.11	Metrics Management Plan		O	O	O	X
2.12	Configuration Management		O	O	O	X
Project Execution						
3.1	Meeting Agenda		X	X	X	X
3.2	Meeting Minutes		X	X	X	X
3.3	Project Status Update Report		O	X	X	X
3.4	Issues Resolution Form		O	O	X	X
3.5	Issues Control Log		O	O	X	X
3.6	Change Request Form		O	O	X	X
3.7	Change Control Log		O	O	X	X
3.8	Metrics Tracking		O	O	X	X
Project Closing						
4.1	Post Project Survey		O	X	X	X
4.2	Post Project Review Report		O	X	X	X
4.3	Project Metrics Report		O	O	X	X

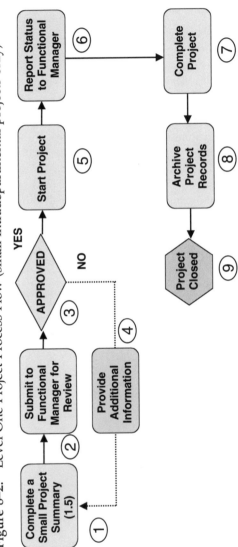

Figure 8–2.   Level One Project Process Flow (small intradepartmental projects only)

Table 8–5. Process Step Description: Level One Project Process Flow Diagram

Step	Step Definition	Role(s)	Activity Definition
1	Complete a Small Project Summary	Project Manager	The first step in the process, after the functional (department) manager assigns the project to one of the department staff to manage, is for the person assigned to fill out the Small Project Summary (1.5).
2	Submit to Functional Manager for Review	Project Manager	The project manager reviews the completed Small Project Summary form with the functional manager to ensure the information is complete and accurate before starting the work required.
3	Approved	Functional Manager	The functional manager gives the approval to proceed with the project work if the information is complete and accurate. If not, the project manager may be required to provide additional information or clarify the information contained on the form. The project manager and functional manager establish and agree upon the frequency and timing of project progress reporting.
4	Provide Additional Information	Project Manager	Additional information or clarifications may be required by the functional manager to ensure that the information contained on the form is accurate and complete enough for future reference.

continued

Table 8–5. *(Continued)*

Step	Step Definition	Role(s)	Activity Definition
5	Start Project	Project Manager	Work can begin on the project only after the Small Project Summary form is complete and the functional manager has given approval for the work to start.
			The project manager submits a copy of the approved Small Project Summary to the PMCoE so it can be used as a reference for other departments. The PMCoE does not record or track Level One project status.
6	Report Status to Functional Manager	Project Manager	The project manager reports progress on the project to the Functional Manager by submitting updated copies of the Small Project Summary form as often as agreed upon in step 3.
7	Complete Project	Project Manager	The project is complete when all the agreed upon work has been completed and deliverables have been met. This includes any testing, training, and implementation that was identified in the Small Project Summary.
8	Archive Project Records	Project Manager	The project records are moved to an archive folder designated by the functional manager.
9	Project Closed	Functional Manager	A post project review meeting is held at the discretion of the functional manager.

Table 8–6. RRAA Matrix: Level One Project Process Flow Diagram

Role	Responsibility	Accountability	Authority
Functional Manager	Creates a department project list, plans, prioritizes, and assigns projects to department project managers. Works with project managers to effectively apply the PMMG tools required to manage the project.	Maintains the project list showing the status of work-in-progress and provides copies to the PMCoE on a monthly basis. Provides administrative and technical direction for department projects.	Reassigns projects-in-progress to other project managers on an as-needed basis. Requests the PMCoE to modify or develop new PMMG tools for managing department projects.
Project Manager	Understands the proper and effective use of the PMMG tools and applies them to manage assigned projects.	Reports project status to the functional manager on an agreed upon frequency.	Requests administrative and/or technical direction. Requests approval of scope changes that affect project deliverables and timing.
PMCoE	Maintains and updates the PMMG and provides training and support for the proper and effective use of the processes, tools, and templates.	Consults with functional managers on the development of new or improved versions of the PMMG processes and tools.	Receives copies of the department project list showing the status of work-in-progress on a monthly basis. Establishes a reference archive to store project documents for learning purposes.

CHAPTER 9

Project Authorization

Section Overview

Project authorization includes a core process to facilitate authorization of new projects to ensure the uses of organization resources are in alignment with its strategic planning goals and objectives. The following is a list of key activities that typically will occur during this process.

- Project Profile
- Project Budget
- Project Portfolio Report

Project Request

The process to authorize a project begins with someone submitting a project profile request form to the PMCoE. Department managers typically file project requests and they often also serve as the project sponsor. The project authorization team reviews the request to determine if it is included in the current forecast plan. If the requested project is not included in the current forecast plan, additional information may be required to approve its addition to the plan. The project portfolio is updated and reports are issued to executive management. Table 9–1 is a list of templates used to complete the requirements for this process.

The Process Flow Diagram, Process Step Description table, and Process RRAA Matrix for this core process are contained in Figure 9–1 and Tables 9–3 and 9–4 of this section.

Table 9–1. Templates/Tools—Project Authorization

ID	Template Name	When Used
1.0	Project Profile	Level 3-4-5
1.8	Budget Worksheet	Level 3-4-5
1.11	Project Portfolio Management Report	Level 3-4-5
	Can also be used for Strategic Forecast Plan	

Project Charter

This process identifies the steps required to add new projects resulting from business opportunities that arise after the master annual project portfolio list has been developed. The process establishes the steps required for project review, approval, and prioritization. Table 9–2 is a list of templates used to complete the requirements for this core process.

Figure 9–1. Project Authorization Process—Level 2 Through Level 5

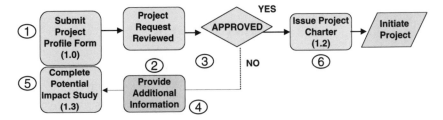

Table 9–2. Templates/Tools—Project Charter

ID	Template Name	When Used
1.2	Project Charter	Level 3-4-5
1.4	Preliminary Communication Plan	Level 3-4-5
1.7	Project Plan (Milestone Level Only)	Level 2-3-4-5
1.8	Budget Worksheet	Level 2-3-4-5
1.9	Scope Statement	Level 2-3-4-5

Table 9–3. Process Step Description: Project Authorization Process—Level 2 Through Level 5

Step	Step Definition	Role(s)	Activity Definition
1	Submit Project Profile Form	Requester	Requests approval to proceed with a new project by submitting a project profile to the PMCoE.
2	Project Request Reviewed	PMCoE	Submits the project profile to the Project Authorization Team (PAT) for review and approval.
3	Approved/Denied	PAT	Determines if the proposed project is included in the current project portfolio.
4	Denied—Provided Additional Information	Requester	PAT asks for additional information or denies the project with justification for the decision.
5	Complete Potential Impact Study	Requester	Obtains additional information requested by the PAT to obtain approval and resubmits the request to the PAT
6	Approved—Issue Project Charter	PMCoE	Prepares a project charter with the input of the project sponsor. The project charter is issued to provide formal authorization for the project to proceed.

Table 9–4. RRAA Matrix: Project Authorization Process—Level 2 Through Level 5

Role	Responsibility	Accountability	Authority
Requester	Submits project documents to the project authorization team (PAT) for review and approval.	Provides additional information or clarifications to the PAT as required for approval.	Receives justification for projects that are rejected.
Project Authorization Team (PAT) (PMCoE Manager plus others to be determined)	Reviews proposed projects to determine if they are worthy of allocating the organization resources.	Establishes and prioritizes an annual master project portfolio list of prioritized projects.	Approves or rejects proposed projects for authorization to proceed with the expenditure of resources.
PMCoE	Manages the project authorization process and assists project requesters to prepare project profiles to request new project authorization.	Maintains the project portfolio and assists the PAT in the project review process.	Requires all projects to follow the project authorization process.

CHAPTER 10

Project Initiation

Section Overview

Project initiation is a core process to facilitate a review and approval of the project Scope Statement and Preliminary Plan by the customer, sponsor, and PMCoE before proceeding to the planning phase. It is during the planning phase of a project that the business requirements are clearly defined and alternative solutions are investigated with the project customer. The functional department manager determines the skill requirements for the project and selects the project manager and team members. The functional department manager also identifies project stakeholders and selects project steering team members. The following activities typically occur during this beginning phase of a project.

- Prepare a preliminary communication plan
- Review business requirements
- Investigate alternative solutions
- Prepare a short project summary (Level one project only)
- Prepare a project scope statement
- Create a preliminary project plan
- Update the estimated project budget
- Define project skills requirements
- Prepare project CAR (if required)

Project Initiation Process

This process identifies the steps required to begin the initiation phase of a project. Information is gathered from the project customer

Table 10–1.   Templates/Tools—Project Initiation

ID	Template Name	When Used
1.2	Project Charter	Level 3-4-5
1.3	Potential Impact	Level 3-4-5
1.4	Preliminary Communication Plan	Level 3-4-5
1.5	Small Project Summary	Level 1 only
1.7	Project Plan (milestone level)	Level 2-3-4-5
1.8	Budget Worksheet	Level 3-4-5
1.9	Scope Statement	Level 2-3-4-5
1.10	Readiness Checklist (define requirements)	Level 3-4-5

to begin a project scope statement, create a preliminary project plan, update the estimated project budget (if required), and complete a CAR (if capital funds are required). Specific skill requirements for the project are also identified at this time to help select the right project team members. These documents are reviewed and signed off by the PMCoE, project customer, and sponsor to obtain approval to proceed to the planning phase. Table 10–1 lists the templates used to complete this process. Figure 10–1 shows the process flow diagram, Table 10–2 shows the process step description, and Table 10–3 contains the RRAA Matrix.

Note: project managers are encouraged, but not required, to use the templates marked *optional*. These tools are provided to facilitate the process of identifying and analyzing project business requirements.

Figure 10–1.   Project Initiation Process

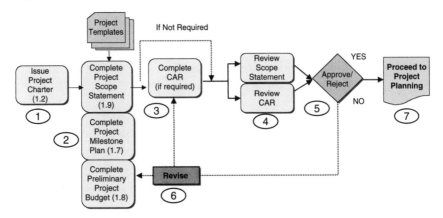

Table 10–2. Process Step Description: Project Initiation Process

Step	Step Definition	Role(s)	Activity Definition
1	Issue Project Charter	PMCoE	The PMCoE issues the project charter, which provides formal recognition for the project and allows it to proceed.
2	Complete Project Scope Statement, Create Preliminary Project Plan, and Update Estimated Project Budget	Project Manager	Prepares a project scope statement, creates the preliminary project plan, and updates the estimated project budget to incorporate any new information that has become available since the project was authorized.
3	Complete CAR (if required)	Project Manager	If capital funds are being requested, the project manager must complete the CAR process.
4	Review Scope Statement/ Review CAR	PMCoE, Financial Controls	The project manager submits the completed scope statement, preliminary project plan, and estimated project budget to the PMCoE for review, comment, and sign-off. The CAR is submitted to financial controls for review, comment, and sign-off. Once these two reviews are completed the scope statement and CAR are submitted to the project customer and sponsor for review, comment, and sign-off.
5	Approve	PMCoE	The PMCoE reviews and approves project scope statements for completeness and clarity. Submittals may be accepted as is or additional information or modifications may be required for approval.
6	Revise	Project Manager	The project manager provides additional information or modifications to the documents as required.
7	Proceed to Project Planning	Project Manager	The project manager follows the steps required in the project planning phase before proceeding with any work on the project.

Table 10–3. RRAA Matrixes: Project Initiation Process

Role	Responsibility	Accountability	Authority
Project Sponsor	Prepares the project charter	Provides formal recognition of the project.	Has authority to approve the project and authorize the next step.
Project Manager	Prepares and submits project scope statement, preliminary project plan, project estimated budget, and CAR (if required).	Submits initiation process documents to the PMCoE, project customer, and project sponsor, and financial controls for review and approval.	Requests input from the project customer and sponsor to complete initiation process documents. Requests assistance from the PMCoE and financial controls to complete initiation process documents.
PMCoE	Reviews and approves initiation process documents.	Assists project managers in the proper completion of initiation process documents.	Maintains and oversees the proper application of the initiation process steps on all projects.
Financial Controls	Reviews and approves CAR process documents.	Assists project managers in the proper completion of CAR process documents.	Maintains and oversees the proper application of the CAR process steps on all projects.
Project Customer and Project Sponsor	Provide input to the development of the initiation process and CAR documents.	Review and approve the initiation process and CAR documents.	Request clarification and modifications to the initiation process and CAR documents before they are approved.

CHAPTER 11

Project Planning

Section Overview

Project planning is a core process that ensures that adequate planning is completed for all projects before work begins. The process begins with the formation of the project team and steering team. The project's classification establishes what core processes need to be put in place for a readiness check, which is the final review and approval step prior to beginning work on a project. The following typically occur during this process.

- Form project team
- Form steering team
- Hold kick-off meeting
- Review scope statement
- Define roles, responsibilities, accountability, and authority
- Establish core processes required by project classification (see Table 8–2 in Chapter 8.)
- Perform readiness check

Project Planning Process

The planning process includes the steps required to ensure that controlling processes are established to monitor and manage the actual work of the project. Table 11–1 lists the templates that are typically used during this phase of the project. Figure 11–1 shows the process flow diagram, Table 11–2 shows the process step descriptions, and Table 11–3 contains the RRAA Matrix for this process.

Table 11–1.   Templates/Tools—Project Planning

ID	Template Name	When Used
2.1	Process Analysis	Level 3-4-5
2.2	Voice of the Customer	Level 3-4-5
2.3	Critical to Quality	Level 3-4-5
2.4	Business Requirements	Level 3-4-5
2.5	Alternate Solutions	Optional
1.7	Project Plan (develop baseline)	Level 2-3-4-5
2.6	Records Administration	Level 2-3-4-5
2.7	RRAA Matrix	Level 3-4-5
2.8	Communication Plan	Level 3-4-5
2.9	Risk Assessment	Level 4-5
2.10	Skills Matrix	Optional
2.11	Metrics Management Plan	Level 4-5
2.12	Configuration Management	Level 4-5

Figure 11–1.   Project Planning Process

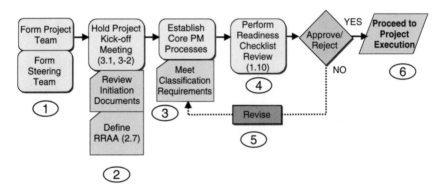

Table 11–2. Process Step Description: Project Planning Process

Step	Step Definition	Role(s)	Activity Definition
1	Form Project and Steering Teams	Project Manager	Project team members and steering team members are asked to participate in the project.
2	Hold Project Kick-off Meeting	Project Manager	A project kick-off meeting is held to review the project initiation documents and to define the roles, responsibilities, accountability, and authority of all project participants.
3	Establish Core PM Processes	Project Manager	Core project management processes (requirements defined by classification) are reviewed with the team and put in place. The project manager schedules the project readiness review with the PMCoE.
4	Perform Readiness Checklist Review	PMCoE	The PMCoE performs the project readiness checklist review with the full project team.
5	Approve	PMCoE	Approval is given to proceed to the implementation of project execution core processes. Any corrective actions determined necessary are identified and completed before approval is provided and a follow-up review is scheduled if necessary.
6	Proceed to Project Execution	Project Team	The project team implements execution core processes and begins working on the tasks to complete the project.

Table 11-3. RRAA Matrix: Project Planning Process

Role	Responsibility	Accountability	Authority
Project Manager	Provides leadership and direction to the project team in the establishment of core project management processes to meet classification requirements. Participates in the selection of third party suppliers. Schedules the readiness checklist review meeting with the PMCoE.	Answers for the project team in the readiness checklist review.	Functions as primary contact with third party suppliers. Can request the PMCoE to approve modifications to readiness requirements if the team believes they are excessive.
Project Team Members	Work with the project manager to establish required project management core processes and prepare for the readiness checklist review.	Provide input during the development of the project baseline plan. Commit to and signoff on the project baseline plan. Become familiar with the required project management core processes.	Request adjustments to the project baseline plan before signing off. Request training in project management core processes if needed.
PMCoE	Chairs the readiness checklist review meeting. Ensures required core project management processes are in place and their proper use is understood prior to granting approval to proceed.	Assists the project team in developing the baseline plan and establishing other required core project management processes.	Requires the use of core project management processes or approves modifications to fit the project when deemed appropriate.

CHAPTER 12

Project Execution

Section Overview

Project Execution includes several core project management processes that monitor and report progress of projects that have passed a readiness check and are approved to proceed. The following activities typically occur during this phase of the project.

- Create and maintain progress reporting cycle
- Establish and maintain steering team reporting cycle
- Institute variance countermeasure planning
- Implement issues resolution process
- Establish project change control procedures
- Perform variance risk assessment
- Carry out metrics tracking

Project Progress Reporting Cycle Process

The project progress reporting cycle process establishes a regularly scheduled reporting day and time, identifies what will be reported, and specifies the format to be used for the project team and steering team review meetings. Table 12–1a lists the templates used during this process. Figure 12–1 shows the process flow diagram, Table 12–1b shows the process step description, and Table 12–1c contains the RRAA matrix.

Table 12–1a.   Templates/Tools—Project Progress Reporting

ID	Template Name	When Used
3.1	Meeting Agenda	Level 2-3-4-5
3.2	Meeting Minutes	Level 2-3-4-5
3.3	Project Status Update Report	Level 3-4-5

Figure 12–1.   Project Reporting Cycle Process

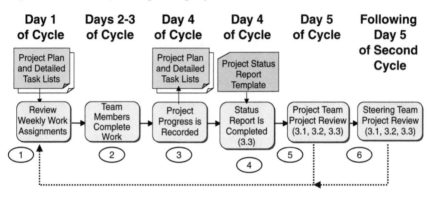

Project Issues Resolution Process

The purpose of the issues resolution process is to identify, assign, track, and report project issues until they are resolved. An issue should be formalized and documented whenever a question or problem cannot be answered or resolved by the originator within a 24-hour period. Any project stakeholder can be an issue originator by completing an Issues Resolution Request Form and submitting it to the person assigned to administrate the issues resolution process. The issues administrator updates the Issues Log, which is reviewed by the project manager and selected members of the team on a weekly basis. Unresolved critical issues are reviewed during project team meetings and steering team meetings. Table 12–2a lists the templates used during this process. Figure 12–2 shows the process flow diagram, Table 12–2b shows the process step description, and Table 12–2c contains the RRAA matrix.

Table 12–1b. Process Step Description: Project Progress Reporting Process

Step	Step Definition	Role(s)	Activity Definition
1	Review Weekly Work Assignments	Project Manager	The project manager provides each team member an assignment list (report generated from the project plan or otherwise created by the project manager).
2	Team Members Complete Work	Team Members	Project team members complete the tasks according to the project plan and/or as assigned during the Day 1 planning meeting.
3	Project Progress Is Recorded	Team Members, Project Manager	Project team members mark up their respective task assignment list to report task actual start and end dates and also estimated percentage completed of work-in-progress tasks. The marked-up list is returned to the project manager by noon of Day 4. The project manager marks up a copy of the project plan to incorporate the individual team member status updates.
4	Status Report Is Completed	Project Manager	The project manager meets with team member(s) whose tasks indicate a variance that will cause slippage in the plan to develop a countermeasure to eliminate or reduce the slippage. The project manager produces the project status report that includes current variances to the plan with countermeasures, unresolved issues, and the status of pending change requests. This report is sent to the PMCoE and the steering team members.
5	Project Team Review	Project Manager	The project manager leads a progress review meeting with all project team members present reporting on plan variances and countermeasure plans, unresolved issues, and pending change requests from their respective functions. Action items are assigned as needed. Minutes of the meeting are recorded to identify outcomes of countermeasure reviews, and action item assignments. The minutes are distributed via e-mail and stored in the WAN project records folders.
6	Steering Team Project Review	Project Manager	The project manager chairs the bimonthly steering team project review meeting. Critical plan variances, countermeasure plans, unresolved issues, and pending change requests requiring steering team assistance to close are discussed. Meeting minutes are recorded, filed, and distributed via e-mail.

Table 12–1c.   RRAA Matrix: Project Progress Reporting Process

Role	Responsibility	Accountability	Authority
Project Manager	Facilitates the completion of work by assisting with the development of variance countermeasure plans, resolves issues, resolves pending change requests. Chairs regular project progress update meetings with the project team.	Provides leadership and direction to the project team. Identifies project schedule variances and develops countermeasures to eliminate or reduce project plan slippages and report same. Resolves functional issues. Reviews and provides input on change requests. Accepts overall responsibility for the project's timely completion to budget and plan. Reports project progress to the steering team on a regular basis.	Holds team members accountable for the timely completion of assigned tasks. Expedites unresolved issues and request for changes to steering team for assistance and approval.
Team Members	Complete assigned work in a timely manner. Attend project progress review meetings.	Report status on work assigned each week.	Request clarification of work assignment requirements. Request assistance to complete assigned tasks.
Steering Team	Provides assistance to resolve critical issues and pending change requests. Expedites requests for assistance to CMT when needed.	Attend and actively participate in project progress update meetings.	Holds the project manager and team accountable for the timely completion of the project within budget.

Table 12–2a. Templates/Tools—Project Issues
Resolution

ID	Template Name	When Used
3.4	Issues Resolution Form	Level 4-5
3.5	Issues Resolution Log	Level 4-5

Figure 12–2. Project Issues Resolution Process

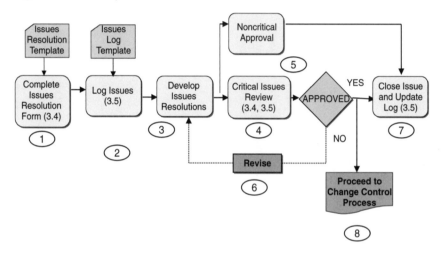

Project Change Control Process

The purpose of the change control process is to identify, record, an-alyze, track, approve, and implement project change requests. The following templates are used during this phase of the project. Table 12–3a lists the templates used during this process. Figure 12–3 shows the process flow diagram, Table 12–3b shows the process step de-scription, and Table 12–3c contains the RRAA matrix. An example of the metrics tracking template can be found in Appendix B.

Note: Metrics tracking is associated with the change control process because the data resulting from project elements that are being measured will often indicate a need to change the process be-ing measured to remove unwanted results or improve performance.

Table 12–2b. Process Step Description: Project Issues Resolution Process

Step	Step Definition	Role(s)	Activity Definition
1	Complete Issues Resolution Form	Originator	The originator identifies an issue by completing an Issues Resolution Form and providing pertinent information about the issue. The form is e-mailed to the person assigned to administer the issues resolution process and the project manager.
2	Log Issues	Administrator	The issues resolution administrator files the Issues Resolution Form, assigns the issue an identification number, and enters it in the Issues Log. The project manager assigns team member(s) to develop a resolution to the issue. The project manger updates the Issues Log with the assignment(s).
3	Develop Issues Resolution	Project Team	The team member(s) develop a resolution to the issue and e-mails it to the project manager for review.
4	Critical Issues Review	Project Manager	The project manager holds a critical issues review meeting with selected project team members to review critical issue resolution progress and discuss proposed solutions.
5	Noncritical Resolution Approval	Project Manager	The project manager reviews noncritical issue resolutions and either accepts them or requests additional solutions. Critical issues are brought to the project team project progress review meetings for discussion.
6	Approve Resolution	Project Team	The project team discusses critical issues and proposed solutions during the project progress review meetings.
7	Close Issue and Update Log	Administrator	Issue resolutions approved by the project manager and the teams are closed and the Issues Log is updated. Some issue resolutions result in a need to proceed with a project change request.
8	Proceed to Change Control Process	Project Manager	Issue resolutions requiring project changes follow the project change control process.

Table 12–2c. RRAA Matrix: Project Issues Resolution Process

Role	Responsibility	Accountability	Authority
Originator	Anyone can establish that an issue exists. The issue originator completes all the required fields on the Issues Resolution Form and e-mails a copy to the project manager.	The issue originator should include sufficient details to clearly identify the problem and what effect it has on the project. The issue originator is often asked to participate in the development of the resolution solution.	The originator can request assistance from other team members to develop issue resolution solutions.
Issues Administrator	The person assigned to administrate the issues resolution process is responsible for entering and closing issues in the Issues Log. In most cases the project manager performs this role.	Maintains the Issues Log and distributes hard copy reports on an as needed basis.	The administrator can request additional information for clarification or incomplete fields on the Issues Resolution Form.
Project Team Member	Team members assist in the development of issues resolution solutions, review, and discuss cross-functional issues.	Provides input to the development of solutions and the approval process.	Requests additional solutions be developed if the proposed solution is not sufficient to resolve the issue.
Project Manager	Reviews and approves noncritical issue resolution solutions. Critical issues are those that impact multiple functions.	Ensures that issues are reviewed and resolved in a timely manner.	Can expedite critical issue to the steering team for its assistance if deemed appropriate.
Steering Team	Reviews critical issues facing the team on a regular basis.	Provides assistance in resolving critical issues that have been expedited to the steering team.	Review and recommend critical issue solution expedited to the Steering Team. Can expedite critical issues to the CMT level if deemed necessary.

Table 12–3a.   Templates/Tools—Project Change
Control

ID	Template Name	When Used
3.6	Change Request Form	Level 4-5
3.7	Change Control Log	Level 4-5

Figure 12–3.   Project Change Control Process

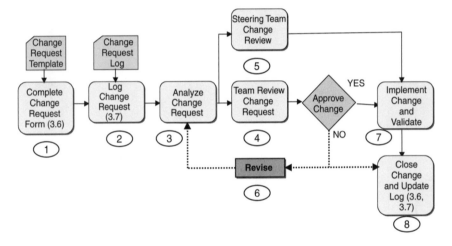

Table 12–3b. Process Step Description: Project Change Control Process

Step	Step Definition	Role(s)	Activity Definition
1	Complete Change Request Form	Originator	Anyone involved in the project (including customers) can request a change by completing an electronic Change Request Form. The completed form is e-mailed to the process administrator and the project manager.
2	Log Change Request	Administrator	The person assigned to administrate the project change control process assigns an Identification Number and enters it into the Change Request Log.
3	Analyze Change Request	Project Manager	The project manager reviews the change request and determines who needs to be involved in the analysis of the request and distributes the change request form via e-mail.
4	Team Review Change Requests	Project Team	The project manager reviews change requests with the team members, asking for their recommendations for approval or denial.
5	Steering Team Change Review	Project Manager	If the change affects cost, time, or quality the change request is brought to the steering team for its review and recommendation for action.
6	Approve Change	Project Manager	The project manager determines if the change request is approved or denied. Change requests may require additional information, in which case additional analysis will be performed. If denied, the change request is closed and the log is updated. The project manager informs the change request originator of the approval/denial decision.
7	Implement Change & Validate	Project Team	Implementation of approved changes is assigned to a team member who coordinates the implementation, validates that it has been completed, and determines that it has met the results intended. The change implementation coordinator closes the change and informs the administrator via e-mail.
8	Close Change & Update Log	Change Coordinator	The change coordinator updates the Change Request Log.

Table 12–3c. RRAA Matrix: Project Change Control Process

Role	Responsibility	Accountability	Authority
Originator	The change request originator must complete the form used to analyze, review, and approve the request.	The originator must provide all the information required in sufficient detail to allow for a timely analysis, review, and approval decision.	The originator can request a business justification that supports the decision to deny a change request.
Administrator	Maintains and updates the Change Request Log file.	Updates the log file in a timely manner and issues hard copy reports when needed.	Requests additional information or clarification from the originator or analysts to complete the Change Request Form.
Project Manager	Assigns team members to analyze requirements and impacts, reviews analysis results with project team and steering team when appropriate.	Facilitates a timely resolution to change requests. Informs the originator of approval/denial decision with a business justification to support the decision.	Obtains input from the project team and steering team to determine the best course of action and approves/denies the change request.
Project Team	Participates in the analysis activity, if assigned, and participates in the review of the request.	Provides a recommendation to the project manager for approval/ denial of the change request supported by a business justification.	Requests that the steering team review the change request before an approval decision is made by the project manager.
Steering Team	Reviews change requests submitted by the project manager.	Provides recommendation for approval/denial to the project manager with supporting business justification.	Reviews all change requests that affect project cost, timing, or quality.

Table 12–4.   Templates/Tools—Metrics Tracking

ID	Template Name	When Used
3.8	Metrics Tracking	Level 4-5

CHAPTER 13

Project Closing

Section Overview

Project closing includes core processes that ensure an orderly, controlled completion of projects. The following activities typically occur during this phase of the project.

- Obtain customer acceptance of deliverables
- Validate third party supplier contact closure
- Balance the project budget
- Close the CAR (covered in the CAR process)
- Hold post project review meeting
- Document lessons learned

Post Project Review Process

A post project review survey is distributed to project participants (i.e., project team members, steering team members, customers, suppliers, and other stakeholders) to gather their individual evaluations of various aspects of the project. The survey responses are compiled and summarized in a report that is distributed and reviewed by the project team in a post project review meeting. The Post Project Review Survey Report is used to facilitate a discussion on lessons learned—what worked and what could be improved upon. The lessons learned are documented and entered into a project knowledge database to allow for keyword searches and easy retrieval by future project teams. They are also used as a basis for evaluation and implementation of process improvements. Table 13–1a lists the templates used during this process. Figure 13–1 shows the process flow diagram, Table 13–1b shows the process step description, and Table 13–1c contains the RRAA matrix.

Metrics Reporting Process

Project measurements that have been collected during project execution are compiled into a report used to validate whether customer expectations were satisfied and that expected benefits have been or will be achieved. Table 13–2a lists the templates used during this process. Figure 13–2 shows the process flow diagram, Table 13–2b shows the process step description, and Table 13–2c contains the RRAA matrix.

Table 13–1a.   Templates/Tools—Post Project Review

ID	Template Name	When Used
4.1	Post Project Survey	Level 3-4-5
4.2	Post Project Review Report	Level 3-4-5

Figure 13–1.   Post Project Review Process

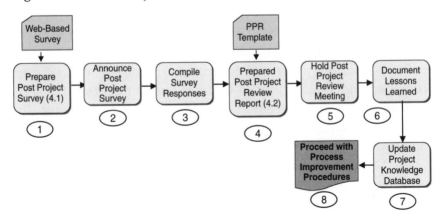

Table 13–1b. Process Step Description: Post Project Review Process

Step	Step Definition	Role(s)	Activity Definition
1	Prepare Post Project Survey	PMCoE	The generic survey instrument is modified to suit the project. The survey is posted to the PMCoE Web site.
2	Announce Post Project Survey	PMCoE	Project participants are invited to complete the survey within a stated period of time and are informed of its location on the PMCoE Web site.
3	Compile Survey Results	PMCoE	The survey responses are compiled and analyzed.
4	Prepare Post Project Review Report	PMCoE	The results are documented in a Post Project Review Report utilizing a report template whose format and table of contents has been standardized.
5	Hold Post Project Review Meeting	PMCoE	The PMCoE schedules and facilitates a post project review meeting, which includes members of the project team and the steering team.
6	Document Lessons Learned	PMCoE	The PMCoE documents lessons learned utilizing a standard template.
7	Update Project Knowledge Database	PMCoE	The PMCoE enters only unique lessons learned into the project knowledge database and files the project lessons learned document with the rest of the project documents. These are archived for future reference.
8	Proceed with Process Improvement Procedures	PMCoE	Lessons learned are evaluated to determine if current processes need to be revised to incorporate recommended improvements, in which case the proper procedures are followed.

Table 13–1c. RRAA Matrix: Post Project Review Process

Role	Responsibility	Accountability	Authority
PMCoE	Prepares, analyzes, interprets, and distributes the post project survey responses in the form of a report. Updates the project knowledge database with new, unique project lessons learned.	Holds a post project review meeting and presents a report and lessons learned.	Presents an objective evaluation of the project from the perspective of the survey responses.
Project Team Members	Complete the post project review survey and attend the follow-up meeting.	Complete the survey within the time allotted and provide honest responses. Participate in the lessons learned discussion.	Make recommendations for process improvements.
Steering Team Members	Complete the post project review survey and attend the follow-up meeting.	Complete the survey within the time allotted and provide honest responses. Participate in the lessons learned discussion.	Make recommendations for process improvements.
Project Stakeholders	Complete the post project review survey and attend the follow-up meeting.	Complete the survey within the time allotted and provide honest responses. Participate in the lessons learned discussion.	Make recommendations for process improvements.
Project Suppliers	Complete the post project review survey.	Complete the survey within the time allotted and provide honest responses.	Offer recommendations for process improvements from the supplier's perspective.

Table 13–2a. Templates/Tools—Metrics Reporting

ID	Template Name	When Used
4.3	Project Metrics Report	Level 4-5

Figure 13–2. Metrics Reporting Process

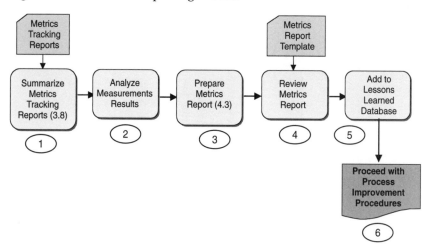

Table 13–2b. Process Step Description: Post Project Review Process

Step	Step Definition	Role(s)	Activity Definition
1	Summarize Metrics Tracking Reports	PMCoE	Summarizes the metrics measurements reported at the end of each project phase.
2	Analyze Measurement Results	PMCoE	Analyzes the actual measurements and compares to baseline objectives.
3	Prepare Metrics Report	PMCoE	Prepares a report that compares the overall measurements to baseline objectives.
4	Review Metrics Report	PMCoE	Presents the report during the post project review meeting.
5	Add to Project Knowledge Database	PMCoE	Updates the project knowledge database with the project metrics.
6	Proceed with Process Improvement Procedures	PMCoE	Applies the metrics results as input for process improvements.

Table 13–2c. RRAA Matrix: Post Project Review Process

Role	Responsibility	Accountability	Authority
PMCoE	Prepares, analyzes, and interprets project metrics measurements, and prepares a report. Records the measurements in the project knowledge database.	Presents the metrics report at the post project review meeting.	Holds the project manager accountable for submitting metrics tracking reports according to a predetermined plan.
Project Manager	Submits metrics tracking reports to the PMCoE according to a predetermined plan.	Compile metrics measurements into periodic tracking reports according to a predetermined plan.	Requires project team members to gather metrics measurements according to a predetermined plan.
Project Team Members	Track assigned metrics measurements and report them to the project manager according to a predetermined plan.	Provide analysis, interpretation, and comments on the measurements to the project manager.	Request changes to the metrics plan if it is felt the measurements are too difficult to quantify or are meaningless.

CHAPTER 14

Education and Training

Section Overview

The goal of the management team is to establish modern project management knowledge and skills as a core competency requirement enterprise-wide within its organization. The successful achievement of this aggressive goal requires a well-designed and implemented education and training program. The following documents provide guidelines for the development of an education and training curriculum.

Education and Training Goals

Table 14–1 establishes goals for the three audiences who are the primary participants of the education and training program. The goals address:

- Business objectives
- Performance objectives
- Competencies
- Knowledge
- Skills
- Attitude

Education and Training Requirements

This document contains a list of knowledge elements in a matrix correlated to the four education and training participant

Table 14-1. Education and Training Goals Matrix

Goals	General Population	Team Members	Project Managers	Functional Managers
Business Objectives	Support the goal to establish project management as a core competency and achieve a world-class proficiency.	Support the goal to establish project management as a core competency.	Manage projects that are completed on time and within budget.	Improve project success and productivity. Achieve corporate strategic planning goals and objectives through effective project management practices.
Performance Objectives	Conversant awareness of the PMMG as the IT project management standard.	Consistent application of project management processes as they are documented in the PMMG.	Consistent use of the PMMG to manage projects.	Proactive support of the PMMG on all projects.
Competency	Conversant knowledge of the principles and practices of project management.	Demonstrate effective application of project management processes as contained in the PMMG.	Demonstrate effective application of the PMMG processes to complete projects on time and within budget.	Establish prioritized department project portfolio and effectively utilize the PMMG to manage the work.

Knowledge	Familiarity with project management terms and acronyms.	Working knowledge of project management processes as contained in the PMMG.	Working knowledge of project management processes as contained in the PMMG.	Working knowledge of project management processes as contained in the PMMG.
Skills	Demonstrate a basic understanding of the project management processes.	Demonstrated ability to effectively apply project management processes contained within the PMMG.	Demonstrated ability to effectively lead others in the application of PMMG processes.	Demonstrated ability to effectively support and enforce the application of project management processes contained within the PMMG.
Attitude	Accept management's goal to establish project management practices as a core competency across the organization.	Desire to effectively apply project management practices at a core competency level.	Desire to effectively apply project management practices at a core competency level.	Support and encourage the adoption of project management as core competency organization goal to achieve.

groups—general population, team members, project managers, and management. The document contains three tables:

- Knowledge objectives (Table 14–2)
- Learning objectives (Table 14–3)
- Assessment methods (Table 14–4)

Education and Training Curriculum

This document contains a brief synopsis of core education and training curriculum. The PMCoE Web site provides up-to-date listings of education and training curricula as they are developed and made available to the organization.

- Entry level (Table 14–5)
- Intermediate level (Table 14–6)
- Advanced level (Table 14–7)

Table 14-2. Knowledge Objectives Requirements

Knowledge Element	General Population	Team Members	Project Managers	Management	Knowledge Element Description
General Knowledge					
PM Terminology	X	X	X	X	PM language (terms and acronyms) and definitions
Project Phases and Life Cycles	X	X	X	X	Project, product, and business life cycle definition
PM Framework	X	X	X	X	PMBOK® Guide framework review
Project Roles and Responsibilities		X	X	X	Project stakeholders, organizational influences, system culture and structure
Key Management Skills			X	X	Review general management skills and other influences
PMMG Contents		X	X	X	Review the PMMG
Project Integration Management					
Strategic Planning Process	X	X	X	X	Understand the steps in strategic planning
Project Estimating	X	X	X	X	Estimate task effort and project size techniques
Project Identification	X	X	X	X	Align projects with strategic planning goals and objectives
Project Prioritization			X	X	Establish and use prioritizing requirements
Project Initiation			X	X	PMMG project initiation process application training
CAR Process			X	X	CAR process application training
Project Portfolio Management			X	X	Portfolio management techniques training
Project Authorization Process			X	X	PMMG project authorization process application training

continued

Table 14-2. (Continued)

Knowledge Element	General Population	Team Members	Project Managers	Management	Knowledge Element Description
Project Scope Management					
Critical Success Factors	X	X	X	X	Identify and quantify CSFs
Project Definition	X	X	X	X	Establish the project purpose and description
Roles and Responsibilities	X	X	X	X	Define project participant RRAA
Project Benefits Identification		X	X	X	Identify and quantify project benefits
Project Deliverables		X	X	X	Identify and quantify project deliverables
Requirements Identification		X	X		Identify and quantify project requirements
Scope Change Control		X	X	X	Employ techniques to manage scope changes
Scope Verification			X	X	Formalize acceptance of the project scope
Project Time Management					
Work Breakdown Structure Development		X	X		Define the project work breakdown structure—use of templates
Activity Definition		X	X		Define activities and level of detail
Activity Sequencing		X	X		Identify activity order and relationships
Activity Duration Estimating		X	X		Use activity effort estimating techniques
Schedule Development		X	X		Optimize and set baseline plan
Schedule Control		X	X		Control changes to the project schedule
MS Project Use			X		Basic training in the use of the tool
Project Status Reporting		X	X	X	Develop a reporting cycle

Project Cost Management

Resource Planning	X	X	Determine and manage all resource requirements
Cost Estimating	X	X	Develop strategic plan and project budgets
Cost Budgeting	X	X	Allocate cost to project activities
Cost Control	X	X	Control changes and reporting status

Project Quality Management

Quality Planning	X		Identify relevant project standards
Quality Assurance	X	X	Evaluate performance on a regular basis
Quality Control	X	X	Establish metrics plan, track measurements, and report

Project Human Resource Management

Resource Management	X	X	Perform project management assessment
Skills Assessment	X	X	Perform skill assessment
Team Development	X		Develop group and individual skills
Project Staffing	X	X	Identify skill requirements
Rewards and Recognition	X	X	Establish a reward and recognition plan

Project Communication Management

Communications Planning	X		Prepare project communications plan
Information Distribution	X		Establish project records and systems

continued

Table 14–2. (Continued)

Knowledge Element	General Population	Team Members	Project Managers	Management	Knowledge Element Description
Performance Reporting		X	X	X	Collect, coordinate, review, and report all forms of information
Administrative Closure		X	X	X	Document post project phase reviews and lessons learned
Project Risk Management					
Risk Management Planning		X	X	X	Decide the approach and plan risk management activities
Risk Identification		X	X		Establish list of risks affecting project
Qualitative Risk Analysis		X	X		Determine the probability of risk occurrence
Quantitative Risk Analysis		X	X		Determine impact of risk
Risk Response Planning		X	X		Develop plans to mitigate the risk
Risk Monitoring and Control		X	X	X	Monitor, execute, and evaluate risk reduction efforts
Project Procurement Management					
Procurement Planning			X	X	Establish requirements and specifications
Solicitation			X	X	Obtain quotations/proposals and approvals
Contract Administration			X		Manage contract relationships
Contract Closeout			X	X	Document deliverables, resolve open issues, close contract

Table 14-3. Learning Objectives Requirements

Learning Outcome Objectives
A = Awareness, F = Familiarity, W = Working Knowledge, E = Expert

Knowledge Element	General Population				Team Members				Project Managers				Management			
	A	F	W	E	A	F	W	E	A	F	W	E	A	F	W	E
General Knowledge																
PM Terminology	X					X					X			X		
Project Phases and Life Cycles	X					X					X			X		
PM Framework	X					X						X		X		
Project Roles and Responsibilities							X					X			X	
Key Management Skills												X				X
PMMG Contents	X					X						X			X	
Project Integration Management																
Strategic Planning Process		X				X					X					X
Project Estimating	X						X					X				X
Project Identification	X					X					X					X
Project Prioritization	X				X						X					X
Project Initiation					X						X					X
CAR Process	X				X							X				X
Project Portfolio Management	X				X					X						X
Project Authorization Process	X				X					X						X
Project Scope Management																
Critical Success Factors	X					X						X				X

continued

Table 14-3. (Continued)

Learning Outcome Objectives
A = Awareness, F = Familiarity, W = Working Knowledge, E = Expert

Knowledge Element	General Population				Team Members				Project Managers				Management			
	A	F	W	E	A	F	W	E	A	F	W	E	A	F	W	E
Project Definition	X					X						X				X
Roles and Responsibilities	X						X					X			X	
Project Benefits Identification	X						X					X				X
Project Deliverables							X					X			X	
Requirements Identification							X					X			X	
Scope Change Control							X					X			X	
Scope Verification							X					X			X	
Project Time Management																
Work Breakdown Structure Development						X						X				X
Activity Definition							X					X				X
Activity Sequencing							X					X			X	
Activity Duration Estimating								X				X				X
Schedule Development							X					X			X	
Schedule Control							X					X			X	

continued

Table 14-3. (Continued)

| Knowledge Element | Learning Outcome Objectives A = Awareness, F = Familiarity, W = Working Knowledge, E = Expert |||||||||||||||
| | General Population |||| Team Members |||| Project Managers |||| Management ||||
	A	F	W	E	A	F	W	E	A	F	W	E	A	F	W	E
MS Project Use						X						X			X	X
Project Status Reporting							X					X			X	X
Project Cost Management																
Resource Planning					X						X					
Cost Estimating												X				X
Cost Budgeting												X				X
Cost Control												X				X
Project Quality Management																
Quality Planning						X						X			X	
Quality Assurance							X					X			X	
Quality Control							X					X				X
Project Human Resource Management																
Resource Management											X					X
Skills Assessment											X					X
Team Development											X					X
Project Staffing											X					X
Rewards and Recognition											X					X

continued

Table 14-3. (Continued)

Knowledge Element	General Population				Team Members				Project Managers				Management			
	A	F	W	E	A	F	W	E	A	F	W	E	A	F	W	E
Project Communication Management																
Communications Planning												X				X
Information Distribution												X				X
Performance Reporting												X				X
Administrative Closure												X				X
Project Risk Management																
Risk Management Planning						X						X				X
Risk Identification							X					X				X
Qualitative Risk Analysis							X					X				X
Quantitative Risk Analysis							X					X				X
Risk Response Planning							X					X				X
Risk Monitoring and Control							X					X				X
Project Procurement Management																
Procurement Planning						X					X					X
Solicitation						X					X					X
Contract Administration						X					X					X
Contract Closeout						X					X					X

Learning Outcome Objectives
A = Awareness, F = Familiarity, W = Working Knowledge, E = Expert

Table 14-4. Assessment Methods Requirements

	Learning Assessment Methods															
	N = None, T = Test, R = Review Documents, E = Evaluate Performance															
	General Population				Team Members				Project Managers				Management			
Knowledge Element	N	T	R	E	N	T	R	E	N	T	R	E	N	T	R	E
General Knowledge																
PM Terminology	X				X					X			X			
Project Phases and Life Cycles	X				X					X			X			
PM Framework	X				X					X			X			
Project Roles and Responsibilities	X						X				X		X			
Key Management Skills	X				X					X				X		
PMMG Contents	X						X				X	X			X	X
Project Integration Management																
Strategic Planning Process	X				X						X				X	X
Project Estimating	X					X	X				X				X	X
Project Identification	X				X				X						X	X
Project Prioritization	X				X				X						X	X
Project Initiation	X				X						X	X			X	X
CAR Process	X				X						X	X			X	X
Project Portfolio Management	X				X							X			X	X
Project Authorization Process	X				X							X			X	X

continued

Table 14–4. (Continued)

	Learning Assessment Methods N = None, T = Test, R = Review Documents, E = Evaluate Performance															

Knowledge Element	General Population				Team Members				Project Managers				Management			
	N	T	R	E	N	T	R	E	N	T	R	E	N	T	R	E
Project Scope Management																
Critical Success Factors	X						X				X				X	
Project Definition	X						X				X				X	
Roles and Responsibilities	X						X				X				X	
Project Benefits Identification	X						X				X	X			X	
Project Deliverables	X						X	X			X	X			X	X
Requirements Identification	X						X	X			X				X	X
Scope Change Control	X						X				X	X			X	X
Scope Verification	X						X				X	X			X	X
Project Time Management																
Work Breakdown Structure Development	X					X				X	X		X			
Activity Definition	X					X				X	X		X			
Activity Sequencing	X					X				X	X					
Activity Duration Estimating	X					X				X	X				X	X

Schedule Development	X	X		X	X	X		X
Schedule Control	X	X		X	X	X		X
MS Project Use	X	X		X	X			X
Project Status Reporting	X	X		X	X	X		X
Project Cost Management								
Resource Planning	X	X			X		X	
Cost Estimating	X				X		X	
Cost Budgeting	X	X			X	X	X	X
Cost Control	X	X			X	X	X	X
Project Quality Management								
Quality Planning	X	X			X		X	
Quality Assurance	X	X			X		X	
Quality Control	X	X		X	X	X	X	X
Project Human Resource Management								
Resource Management	X	X			X		X	X
Skills Assessment	X	X			X		X	X
Team Development	X	X			X	X	X	X
Project Staffing	X	X			X	X	X	
Rewards and Recognition	X	X		X	X	X	X	X

continued

Table 14-4. (*Continued*)

Knowledge Element	General Population				Team Members				Project Managers				Management			
	N	T	R	E	N	T	R	E	N	T	R	E	N	T	R	E
Project Communication Management																
Communications Planning	X				X						X	X				X
Information Distribution	X				X						X	X				X
Performance Reporting	X				X						X	X				X
Administrative Closure	X				X						X	X				X
Project Risk Management																
Risk Management Planning	X					X				X	X	X		X	X	X
Risk Identification	X					X				X	X	X		X	X	X
Qualitative Risk Analysis	X					X				X	X	X		X	X	X
Quantitative Risk Analysis	X					X				X	X	X		X	X	X
Risk Response Planning	X					X				X	X	X		X	X	X
Risk Monitoring and Control	X					X				X	X	X		X	X	X
Project Procurement Management																
Procurement Planning	X				X					X	X	X			X	X
Solicitation	X				X					X	X	X			X	X
Contract Administration	X				X					X	X	X			X	X
Contract Closeout	X				X					X	X	X			X	X

Table 14–5. Curriculum Requirements: Entry Level

ID	Course Name	Course Objectives	Topics
1.1	Introduction to Project Management	Introductory class that informs participants what the discipline of project management is all about	Project Management—What is it? The growth of project management Project management methodologies Project management maturity
	Target Audience	All employees	
	Duration	1.0 hour	
	Prerequisites	None	
	Delivery and Media	PowerPoint presentation with notes provided	
1.2	PMCoE Overview	Introductory class to review the Project Management Center of Excellence Charter	Purpose Vision Mission Strategy Goals and objectives Methodology Critical success factors
	Target Audience	All employees	
	Duration	1.0 hour	
	Prerequisites	None	
	Delivery and Media	PowerPoint presentation with notes provided	Roles, responsibilities, accountability, authority

Table 14-6. Curriculum Requirements: Intermediate Level

ID	Course Name	Course Objectives	Topics
2.1	PMMG Review	Introduction to the project management methodology guidelines contents	Introduction Authorization
	Target Audience	Project team members, project managers, functional managers	Initiation Planning Execution
	Duration	1.0 hour	Closing
	Prerequisites	Introduction to project management PMCoE overview	Education and Training
	Delivery and Media	Classroom discussion with copy of PMMG provided to all participants	Templates
2.2	PMMG Processes and Templates	Review of the purpose and use of the PMMG processes and templates	Authorization Master project portfolio and capital budget plan development process
	Target Audience	Project team members, project managers, functional managers	Project request/authorization process Project initiation process
	Duration	2.0 hours	Project planning process Project execution process
	Prerequisites	PMMG review	Progress reporting cycle process Project issues resolution process
	Delivery and Media	Classroom discussion with participants using their own PMMG copies. Examples of some templates used to demonstrate the proper use.	Project change control process Project closing process Post project review process Metrics reporting process

2.3	PM Basic Training Scope and Planning	In-depth review of project scope management and project time management (planning) principles and related processes. Review of the PMMG scope and plan templates with instructions on their proper use.	*Morning Session* Introductions Expectations Introduction to Project scope Scope initiation Scope planning Scope definition Scope verification Scope change Control Review templates Q&A	*Afternoon Session* Introduction to project planning Activity definition Activity sequencing Activity estimating Schedule development Schedule control Performance reporting Review templates Q&A
	Target Audience	Project managers, functional managers		
	Duration	6.0 hours		
	Prerequisites	Introduction to project management PMCoE overview PMCoE review PMMG processes and templates		
	Delivery and Media	PowerPoint presentation and classroom discussion, with notes and examples provided		
2.4	Project Plan Development	A facilitated work session to develop a specific project's plan.	*Session One* Develop work breakdown structure Develop project task list Create network diagram of project plan	*Session Two* Create MS project plan from network diagram Optimize the project plan Establish baseline plan
	Target Audience	Project manager and project team members		
	Duration	2.0–4.0 hours—2 sessions		
	Prerequisites	Introduction to project management PM Basic Training—Scope and Planning		
	Delivery and Media	Facilitated working session using whiteboard, flip charts, and sticky notes to create the network diagram. A laptop and projector are used in the second session to create the MS project plan.		

continued

Table 14–6. *(Continued)*

ID	Course Name	Course Objectives	Topics
2.5	MS Project Training	This course provides basic training in MS project.	TBD
	Target Audience	Project managers, functional managers	
	Duration	4.0 hours	
	Prerequisites	Computer lab training on or off site	
	Delivery and Media	Internal or external classes TBD	
2.6	Process Mapping	A facilitated workshop to develop process mapping for a specific project	Process relationship map
			As-Is process map
			To-Be process map
	Target Audience	Project managers, project team members	Gap analysis
	Duration	4.0 hours (multiple sessions may be required, depending on the complexity of the project)	Action plan
	Prerequisites	None	
	Delivery and Media	Facilitated working session using whiteboard, flip charts, and sticky notes to create the project process maps	
2.7	Project Risk Management	A facilitated workshop to develop risk management for a specific project.	Risk management planning
			Risk identification
	Target Audience	Project managers, project team members	Qualitative risk analysis
	Duration	4.0 hours	Quantitative risk analysis
	Prerequisites	None	Risk response planning
	Delivery and Media	Facilitated working session using whiteboard, flip charts, and sticky notes to create the risk management plan.	Risk monitoring and control

Table 14-7. Curriculum Requirements: Advanced Level

ID	Course Name	Course Objectives	Topics
3.1	Project Management Executive Overview	This presentation is designed to provide executive managers with the information required to implement modern project management best practices as an organizational core competency.	Project management overview Project management—What is it? The growth of project management PMI® project management methodology
	Target Audience	Executive and functional managers	PM organization structure and maturity PMCoE vision, mission and objectives Project management methodology Project management maturity
	Duration	2.0 hours	
	Prerequisites	None	
	Delivery and Media	PowerPoint with notes provided	
3.2	PMP Certification Qualification Preparation	This session is designed to assist participants in preparing the PMP® certification qualification document for submittal to PMI®	*Session One* *Session Two* Review PMI® qualification Complete submittal requirements document Prepare records to support submittal
	Target Audience	Project managers	
	Duration	Two 1.0 hour sessions	
	Prerequisites	See PMI certification qualification requirements	
	Delivery & Media	One-on-one sessions	
3.3	PMP Certification Study	This course is designed to help individuals prepare for taking the PMI® PMP® certification exam.	Session 1—Framework, initiate & close Session 2—Planning core processes Session 3—Planning facilitating processes Session 4—Execution processes Session 5—Closing processes Each session includes example tests and discussion of reference materials
	Target Audience	Project managers	
	Duration	Five 4.0 hour sessions	
	Prerequisites	See PMI® certification qualification requirements	
	Delivery and Media	PowerPoint presentation and classroom discussion, with notes and examples provided	

APPENDIX A

PMCoE Tools

This section contains complete copies of the forms, surveys, and other tools presented in Section I of the book.

PMCoE TOOL INDEX

ID	Description
TL-1	PMCoE Charter
TL-2	Management Team Survey
TL-3	Project Evaluation Survey
TL-4	Project Management Maturity Survey

TL-1 PMCoE CHARTER

Purpose: The Management Team (MT) has determined there is a need to improve the capability for managing projects within the organization. The MT has elected to establish a Project Management Center of Excellence (PMCoE) with the responsibility, accountability, and requisite authority to enable the organization to achieve this strategic objective.

Vision: The organization will achieve a world-class proficiency in the consistent application of common project management standards, processes, and procedures to ensure that quality is incorporated into core business processes and projects.

Mission: To provide the leadership that will enable the organization to manage its programs, projects, services, and support utilizing sound project management methodologies, standards, practices, and procedures. To ensure project management, internal quality, and project gate review processes are adopted enterprise-wide efficiently and effectively as a result of a continuous improvement of project management knowledge, skills, and capability.

Strategy: Create an environment within the organization that supports the alignment of projects with strategic corporate goals and objectives where the organization embraces project management as an intrinsic enabler as it seeks to attain its goals and objectives within the context of its vision, mission, goals, and objectives.

Goals and Objectives: To establish project management practices as the natural means of accomplishing work to the degree it becomes part of the organization's culture. Define and institutionalize project management processes across the organization.

Methodology: Establish a PM network management composed of MT members that function as a forum to discuss project management issues and support PMCoE efforts to satisfy the charter, purpose, vision, mission, goals, and objectives. The PM network members will also participate individually in the development and output of the following teams:

- **Project Review and Authorization:** Responsible for ensuring proposed projects align with organizational strategic goals and objectives. Responsible for developing the requirements for reviewing, evaluating, and approving proposed projects, including business case criteria, proposal format, and development and submittal process. Responsible for the creation and oversight of a project chartering process.

- **Project Management Standards and Methods:** Responsible for identifying and developing the project management standards and methods that include policies, processes, and procedures that will be owned, distributed, monitored, and maintained by the PMCoE.

- **Project Management Education and Training:** Responsible for developing the criteria for a project management education and training program that includes project management career path requirements, curriculum requirements, testing criteria, and validation processes.

- **Project Health Check:** Responsible for reviewing and approving project readiness to proceed by ensuring that applicable project startup process deliverables have been satisfied prior to project start-up as well as establishing readiness prior to the to start of each subsequent project phase.

Critical Success Factors: To ensure a successful startup and continuance of the PMCoE, the following activities must be supported:

- Partner with senior management to plan and dynamically manage the organization's change from what it is now to a new, revitalized organization, where project management (PM) is the primary means of accomplishing the organization's strategic goals and objects and permeates all levels of the organization.
- Management understands and accepts that the PMCoE will be evolving over time, on a consistent pace with the organization's ability to manage the change affecting its PM maturity.
- Management is committed to ensuring the PMCoE is accepted and supported at all levels of the organization.
- Ensure that PMCoE implementation plan is consistent and aligns with corporate goals and objectives.
- Ensure the PMCoE implementation budget is in alignment with funding goals and objectives.
- Ensure deployment of resources is in alignment with corporate goals and objectives.
- Ensure risks associated with the PMCoE implementation are assessed and managed.
- Information, communication, and reporting structure support the PMCoE implementation.
- Mandate and ensure that project planning execution and configuration are consistent with corporate goals and objectives.
- Provide personnel evaluation system that reinforces project management as a team strategy in the company s business philosophy.
- Facilitate project feasibility determination and project initiation of work-in-progress and future work that is defined as "projects." The PMCoE leads and facilitates the evaluation and feasibility of program/project portfolio management as it relates to strategic decision-making in support of new projects during the project initiation phase.
- Define PM core competencies and PM skills as a part of an internal qualification and certification process for project managers within the organization.
- To support the growth and development of the project team staffing, education, and training.
- Provide a home for career path project managers and the project management support staff.
- The PMCoE is responsible for the determination and oversight of "special projects" that are mission critical to the strategic direction of the company or where such projects have or could have a pervasive impact on the corporate goals and objectives.

- The PMCoE ensures the funding gates and limits are consistent with an approved schedule of values.
- The PMCoE leads and facilitates project close-out, lessons learned, process improvement, better estimating, building and using models for strategic decision making.

PMCOE Roles, Responsibilities, Accountability, and Authority: (various capacities)

Leadership Role	Establishment of the IT organization's project management policies, processes, procedures, methodology, standards, skills, capability, maturity and support.
Responsibility	Establish a capability maturity framework through the integration of a project management methodology.
	Establish process development, process management, and process improvement programs as a way of doing business.
	Define the core skills and competencies required.
	Develop education and training programs to facilitate the just-in-time transfer of project management skills and knowledge.
Accountability	Performance attributes and measures shall be established using the project planning process.
Authority	Requisite authority that is sufficient to require conformance to methodology, standards, and skills.
Consulting Role	Facilitate, integrate, and support the development of enterprise-wide information technology in support of the corporate strategies in: • Business systems • Communication • Quality programs • Human resource • Financial management
Responsibility	Codevelop and manage the implementation of sound technology practices that provide the capability for timely distribution of project information across the enterprise.
	Codevelop an in-process quality improvement program that is fully integrated into the planning process and managed accordingly.
	Identify and manage project requirements for: • Capacity (availability and productivity) • Capability (competency development, skills, and training) • Culture (work environment, communication, team building, and compensation)
	Development of project budgets, actual performance and financial forecast in support of the corporate financial systems.
Accountability	Negotiated within the relationship.
Authority	Negotiated within the relationship.
Mentoring Roles	Advance the development of personal growth in project management skills and techniques within the corporate culture.
Responsibility	Facilitate, integrate, and support the transfer of project management skills and core competencies through an organized mentoring program.
Accountability	Honest, open, and caring.
Authority	Not required.

TL-2 Management Team Survey

1	What are your primary role(s) and responsibilities?
2	What types of activities take most of your time?
3	Do documented procedures exist for applying project management processes in your discipline?
4	Do you experience any problems with these processes? If yes, what do you think is the cause of each of these problems?
5	Are the roles and responsibilities of project team members clearly defined and documented?
6	Was a project kick-off meeting held on your project? Do all internal project participants attend these meetings?
7	What are your current project goals?
8	How are project time constraints communicated to you, or from you?

Internally	Externally

9	How are project scope changes communicated to you?
10	Are you directly involved in the development of the project baseline schedule?
11	What project status reporting are you personally responsible for producing and how do you communicate it:

Daily	Weekly	Monthly

12	What kind of estimating (hours, $$, time duration, and so forth) is done in your area?
13	What kinds of estimating tools are used (hardware, software, and processes)?

14	Is your project management role(s) and responsibilities well defined and how were they communicated to you?

15	What is measured on a project: (mark all that apply with an X)

Timing	Quality	Cost	Other	

16	Do you track actual hours and/or costs? If so describe the system, reports, and so forth, that are used.

17	Are project management quality metrics established to capture lessons learned to improve the processes used to manage projects?

18	Do you have proper equipment and tools (software, procedures) to be effective in your job?

19	What do you see as the value of the project management processes?

20	What other management controls do you think are needed?

21	How are project resources selected and assigned?

22	Approximately how much formal project management training have you had?

Estimated time	Sufficient for you?	Individual training plans?

23	Would you like to obtain additional skills to improve your ability to meet project objectives?

24	What skills do you believe are most important for your job?

25	How are strategies communicated throughout the organization?

26	How do you know you are doing the right things and how do your people know it?

27	Who is responsible for communicating plans and schedules in your group?			
	Who		How	When

28	To whom do you report the status of your work (customer, managers, peers, outside groups, suppliers, vendors)?

29	What information are you not getting that you wish you could get on a reliable basis?

30	How successful/useful is the communication? (Mark each with X.)						
	Poor	Fair	Good		Poor	Fair	Good
Between you and your colleagues?				Between you and your direct supervisor?			
Between you and the project manager?				Between the company and the customer?			
On overall project status?				On the objectives of the project?			
On your objectives?				On your performance?			
On project decisions?				On project issues?			
Total Responses				Percentage of total responses			

31	In your view, what is the largest risk to your success on a project?

32	In your opinion, what hampers/enables your organization most to meet on-time delivery?

TL-3 Project Evaluation Survey

Project Name:
Project Owner:
Project Phase:
Project Start Date:
Project Finish Date:

Project Management Requirements (see assessment chart below)	
Integration Management	**Comments**
Constraints/Limitations	
Project Summary	
PM Processes Documented	
Change Control Process	
Configuration Management	
Scope Management	**Comments**
Scope Statement	
Statement of Work	
Work Breakdown Structure	
Baseline Schedule	
Time Management	**Comments**
Resource Breakdown Structure	
Project Schedule	
Tracking/Countermeasures	
Project Status Reports	
Cost Management	**Comments**
Project Budget	
Cost Breakdown Structure	
Quality Management	**Comments**
Metric Collection	
Human Resource Management	**Comments**
Roles / Responsibilities	
Organizational Breakdown Structure	

Communication Management	Comments
Communication Plan	
Project Workbook	
Issues Process	
Risk Management	**Comments**
Risk Assessment	
Procurement Management	**Comments**
Supplier Status Reporting	

Status Symbol Table

1	No process exists	4	Process documented and consistently applied
2	Process exists, not documented	5	Process documented and audited consistently
3	Process exists, documented, but not commonly applied		

TL-4 Project Management Maturity Survey

Date:
Name:
Title:
Department:
Description of primary responsibilities:
List your primary internal customer(s):

Please check all the boxes that apply to you.

Project Management Knowledge

	High	I have formal training and/or extensive experience in applying all or most of the project management functions outlined in this survey.
	Medium	I have read about and/or observed the application of project management principles as defined in this survey, but have not been personally involved in their application.
	Low	I do not know much about project management other than occasionally hearing the phrase or seeing it in print.

Level of Support

	High	I believe that applying project management principles within all areas of our organization is necessary to ensure our continued growth and competitiveness in the marketplace.
	Medium	I think using project management techniques is a good idea, but I am not sure where or how we should apply them in our organization.
	Low	It does not matter to me if we use project management or not, because I don t think it will affect my activities. I am neither for nor against the issue.
	None	I think we are doing just fine now and don t see the need to spend time and money to make any changes in the way we do business.

Thank you for taking the time to answer these questions carefully. They will help us understand how we might help you improve your current business practices for managing projects.

1.0 Integration Management

<u>Responses:</u>
0 = Don't Know, **1** = Never, **2** = Sometimes, **3** = Usually, **4** = Frequently, **5** = Always

Level of Knowledge

ITEM	0	1	2	3	4	5	STATEMENT
1.1							Project constraints are clearly defined by the customer for each project.
1.2							Assumptions are identified and documented prior to addressing project risks.
1.3							Formal organizational policies exist that include quality management, personnel management, and financial controls.
1.4							A project planning methodology is documented and strictly adhered to.
1.5							A *Project Management Information System (PMIS)* is in place, consisting of the tools and techniques used to gather, integrate, and disseminate the outputs of the other project management processes.
1.6							A project charter, giving the project manager authority to apply organizational resources, is used as formal approval to start a project.
1.7							There is an overall change control process to manage scope creep, maintain performance measurement integrity, and coordinate the review, approval, and implementation of approved changes that affect cost, risk, quality, and staffing.
1.8							A documented configuration management procedure is in place to apply technical and administrative direction and surveillance of proper application of the project management methodology.
1.9							A performance measurement criterion has been developed to establish how project progress will be determined and reported during the status update process.
1.10							A post project review process is followed to capture *lessons learned* for incorporation as part of the project management methodology continuous improvement process.
Totals							Determine the average score and enter the result on the scorecard.

Level of Importance

Level	Item(s)	Comments
None		
Low		
Medium		
High		

2.0 Scope Management

Responses:
0 = Don t Know, **1** = Never, **2** = Sometimes, **3** = Usually, **4** = Frequently, **5** = Always

Level of Knowledge

ITEM	0	1	2	3	4	5	STATEMENT
2.1							A Project Scope Statement is created for every project.
2.2							Project Scope Statements are prepared with customer input throughout the development process.
2.3							Management and the customer reviews all project progression alternatives and recommendations.
2.4							The project team and customer review project requirements on a regular basis.
2.5							A Work Breakdown Structure Dictionary (WBSD) containing detailed descriptions of the project s work is created for each project.
2.6							A documented Change Control process is in place for managing changes to the project plan.
2.7							The Statement of Work (SOW) contains all deliverables and is reflected in the Project Plan.
2.8							All project participants endorse the Baseline Project Schedule.
2.9							Potential changes to the Baseline Project Schedule are processed according to a documented Change Control Procedure.
2.10							Approved changes to the Baseline Project Schedule are communicated to the project team and the customer.
Totals							Determine the average score and enter the result on the scorecard.

Level of Importance

Level	Item(s)	Comments
None		
Low		
Medium		
High		

3.0 Time Management

<u>Responses:</u>
0 = Don t Know, **1** = Never, **2** = Sometimes, **3** = Usually, **4** = Frequently, **5** = Always

Level of Knowledge

ITEM	0	1	2	3	4	5	STATEMENT
3.1							The project requirements (deliverables) are reflected in the project s Work Breakdown Structure (WBS).
3.2							The project s WBS and resource estimate are used to develop the project s baseline schedule.
3.3							All project assumptions are documented when developing the project schedule.
3.4							The project schedule identifies schedule constraints driven by the customer, technology, suppliers, or management.
3.5							All project schedule work elements have dependencies, effort, and resources assigned.
3.6							A critical path analysis is performed on the project schedule during each progress update cycle.
3.7							Project schedules are updated on a regular basis with progress status updates, which are measured against the baseline plan.
3.8							Resource-constrained and resource-leveled schedules are created and maintained.
3.9							Schedules are optimized to conform to contract requirements.
3.10							Project team member assignments, responsibilities, and authority are covered in project team kick-off meetings held prior to the start of every project.
Totals							Determine the average score and enter the result on the scorecard.

Level of Importance

Level	Item(s)	Comments
None		
Low		
Medium		
High		

4.0 Cost Management

<u>Responses:</u>
0 = Don t Know, **1** = Never, **2** = Sometimes, **3** = Usually, **4** = Frequently, **5** = Always

Level of Knowledge

ITEM	0	1	2	3	4	5	STATEMENT
4.1							Cost centers are set up to track actual project expenditures against budget for specific line items of the project schedule.
4.2							The project management environment has processes that support gathering of financial data for periodic reports.
4.3							Project financial standards processes and procedures are documented and consistently followed.
4.4							Project team members receive training in financial standards and procedures.
4.5							Project budgets are based on resource estimates and the resource plan.
4.6							Actual costs are tracked and reconciled with the original estimated costs.
4.7							There is a consistent process documenting all estimating and cost assumptions.
4.8							A common list of cost categories exists for all project budgets.
4.9							Contractual issues are documented and closed prior to project sign-off.
4.10							A common documented process is in place for completing all financial procedures required to close a project.
Totals							Determine the average score and enter the result on the scorecard.

Level of Importance

Level	Item(s)	Comments
None		
Low		
Medium		
High		

5.0 Quality Management

Responses:
0 = Don t Know, **1** = Never, **2** = Sometimes, **3** = Usually, **4** = Frequently, **5** = Always

Level of Knowledge

ITEM	0	1	2	3	4	5	STATEMENT
5.1							A documented procedure exists for creating and maintaining a Project Workbook.
5.2							Each project has a Configuration Management Plan.
5.3							Every project has a Quality Assurance Plan.
5.4							The project team reviews all of the processes and procedures that apply prior to the start of every project.
5.5							Common documented processes and procedures for technical performance, business performance, quality, and metrics are applied to every project.
5.6							An initial review of the project plan, involving all participants, is conducted prior to creating a baseline project plan to ensure completeness and consistency.
5.7							On a regular basis, variances are reviewed between the current progress status and project cost against the baseline plan.
5.8							On a regular basis, project trend data are analyzed, based on metrics data.
5.9							An Issues Resolution Process for the project is established and followed.
5.10							A Change Control Process for the project is established and followed.
Totals							Determine the average score and enter the result on the scorecard.

Level of Importance

Level	Item(s)	Comments
None		
Low		
Medium		
High		

6.0 Human Resource Management

Responses:
0 = Don t Know, **1** = Never, **2** = Sometimes, **3** = Usually, **4** = Frequently, **5** = Always

Level of Knowledge

ITEM	0	1	2	3	4	5	STATEMENT
6.1							A Staffing Plan is created and followed for every project.
6.2							Team members are selected to match roles and responsibilities, which are defined and documented.
6.3							The size of the project is determined according to a documented process.
6.4							All project resource needs (such as hardware, software, and space) are clearly documented.
6.5							All estimating process assumptions are documented for each project.
6.6							An Organization Breakdown Structure is created for each project.
6.7							Customer resource requirements for the project are planned and documented.
6.8							Project skills and experience needs are defined and documented consistently.
6.9							The training and developmental needs of all team members are documented.
6.10							A documented process is in place for recognizing outstanding commitments or performance on a project.
Totals							Determine the average score and enter the result on the scorecard.

Level of Importance

Level	Item(s)	Comments
None		
Low		
Medium		
High		

7.0 Communication Management

Responses:
0 = Don t Know, **1** = Never, **2** = Sometimes, **3** = Usually, **4** = Frequently, **5** = Always

Level of Knowledge

ITEM	0	1	2	3	4	5	STATEMENT
7.1							Each project has a committed customer sponsor.
7.2							A strong team atmosphere exists between the project team and the customer.
7.3							A Communication Plan, documenting the required project communications, is created for each project and is followed by the project team.
7.4							A Project Announcement is made to both the customer s organization and yours to increase project awareness.
7.5							After each formal meeting, minutes are prepared and distributed to all affected parties.
7.6							Project status reporting procedures are established and followed.
7.7							Project information is updated and readily accessible to the organization at all times.
7.8							Variance Analysis for schedule, budget, and effort is communicated on a regular basis.
7.9							Project status review meetings are held regularly with company leadership, the customer, and suppliers.
7.10							Project successes are documented for inclusion into a Close-Down Announcement and Success Story.
Totals							Determine the average score and enter the result on the scorecard.

Level of Importance

Level	Item(s)	Comments
None		
Low		
Medium		
High		

8.0 Risk Management

<u>**Responses:**</u>
0 = Don t Know, **1** = Never, **2** = Sometimes, **3** = Usually, **4** = Frequently, **5** = Always

Level of Knowledge

ITEM	0	1	2	3	4	5	STATEMENT
8.1							A high-level risk assessment is completed at the start of each project.
8.2							The high-level risk assessment includes major project characteristics such as size, effort, and cost.
8.3							The high-level risks are rated as low, medium, and high probabilities.
8.4							Project risks are documented using a common format.
8.5							A risk assessment/handling plan is created for large projects.
8.6							Project risks are evaluated for priority, probability, and impact.
8.7							The method for managing each accepted risk is documented.
8.8							Action plans are created for risks to be mitigated or transferred.
8.9							Contingency plans are created for accepted risks.
8.10							Regularly scheduled project status meetings include a review of a project s risks.
Totals							Determine the average score and enter the result on the scorecard.

Level of Importance

Level	Item(s)	Comments
None		
Low		
Medium		
High		

9.0 Procurement Management

Responses:
0 = Don t Know, **1** = Never, **2** = Sometimes, **3** = Usually, **4** = Frequently, **5** = Always

Level of Knowledge

ITEM	0	1	2	3	4	5	STATEMENT
9.1							A standard contract (agreement) that includes language covering project management requirements, such as progress status updating, is issued for project goods and services.
9.2							A procurement plan is in place that identifies what to procure and when is developed at the start of each project.
9.3							Project timing requirements are clearly defined in a formal contract or agreement for purchased goods and services.
9.4							Contract Administration is an integral part of the project management organization.
9.5							A make-buy analysis is performed prior to the start of every project.
9.6							Procurement Management processes have been documented.
9.7							All procurements are identified with the specific project plan WBS task it supports.
9.8							An evaluation process that meets specific criteria has been formalized to provide a consistent method for proposal review and acceptance.
9.9							A contract change control process is in place.
9.10							A contract closeout process that records the evaluation of supplier performance in meeting their contact requirements is documented.
Totals							Determine the average score and enter the result on the scorecard.

Level of Importance

Level	Item(s)	Comments
None		
Low		
Medium		
High		

Survey Summary Evaluation

The AVERAGE Knowledge and Importance scores from each Project Management Body of Knowledge (PMBOK⬚) section on the preceding pages are recorded in the table below. An analysis of the score for each area will quickly reveal the possible maturity level of each area, which can then be prioritized for potential improvement in the organization.

PM Process Maturity Levels: Importance (I) scores are for reference only and not included in the calculations.
LEVEL 1- INITIAL: No formal methodology, no project portfolio management
LEVEL 2 - REPEATABLE: Systemic planning and control with a standard methodology
LEVEL 3 - MANAGED: Merging of product and PM processes
LEVEL 4 - DISTRIBUTED: Integrated PM and business systems
LEVEL 5 - SUSTAINED: Continuous PM process improvement

PMBOK Area	Avg.		LEVEL 1	LEVEL 2	LEVEL 3	LEVEL 4	LEVEL 5
	K	I	0-1.0	1.1-2.0	2.1-3.0	3.1-4.0	4.1-5.0
1.0 Integration							
2.0 Scope							
3.0 Time							
4.0 Cost							
5.0 Quality							
6.0 Human Resource							
7.0 Communication							
8.0 Risk							
9.0 Procurement							

The overall Project Management Maturity Level is:_____
(Total all columns and divide by 9)

APPENDIX B

List of Standard PMMG Templates

File Name	Template Name
PMMG 1-0	Project Profile
PMMG 1-1	Project Selection
PMMG 1-2	Project Charter
PMMG 1-3	Potential Impact
PMMG 1-4	Preliminary Communication Plan
PMMG 1-5	Short Project Summary
PMMG 1-6	Project Summary (See Request/Authorization Process)
PMMG 1-7	Project Plan (MS Project 98 File)
PMMG 1-8	Budget Worksheet
PMMG 1-9	Scope Statement
PMMG 1-10	Readiness Checklist
PMMG 1-11	Project Portfolio Management Report
PMMG 2-1	Process Analysis
PMMG 2-2	Voice of the Customer
PMMG 2-3	Critical to Quality
PMMG 2-4	Business Requirements
PMMG 2-5	Alternative Solutions
PMMG 2-6	Records Administration
PMMG 2-7	RRAA Matrix
PMMG 2-8	Communication Plan
PMMG 2-9	Risk Assessment
PMMG 2-10	Skills Matrix
PMMG 2-11	Metrics Management Plan
PMMG 2-12	Configuration Management
PMMG 3-1	Meeting Agenda
PMMG 3-2	Meeting Minutes
PMMG 3-3	Project Status Update Report
PMMG 3-4	Issues Resolution Form
PMMG 3-5	Issues Control Log
PMMG 3-6	Change Request Form
PMMG 3-7	Change Control Log
PMMG 3-8	Metrics Tracking
PMMG 4-1	Post Project Survey
PMMG 4-2	Post Project Review Report
PMMG 4-3	Project Metrics Report

PMMG 1.0 PROJECT PROFILE   Strategic Forecast Planning

Project ID:		Project Name:	

General Information

Department:		Completed By:	
Department Manager:		Target Launch Date:	

Project Description

Project Rationale

Initiative / Strategy Supported

Project Risk(s) If Not Implemented

Rough Order of Magnitude (Estimated duration of project)

Level	Effort - Hrs	Est. Accuracy H-M-L	Comments

Departments and Systems Impacted

Department	Systems Impacted	L-M-H

Skills Required

Skill Required	Number of Resources

Equipment / Hardware / Software Required

Equipment/Hardware/Software Description	Quantity	Est. Cost

Estimated Project Budget

Cost Description	Estimated Cost

Estimated Savings

Savings Description	Estimated Savings

PMMG 1.1 PROJECT SELECTION

Project ID:		Project Name:	

Instructions: Enter a project description for your project, then evaluate the statement, and modify it (if needed) by using the criteria below. Place an X below or next to the rating selection you feel is most accurate for this project.

Project description:

Criteria	Rating					
This project directly supports a specific corporate goal or objective.	1 A lot	2	3	4	5 No	Don't know
Customer requirements can be clearly defined.	1 Easy	2	3	4	5 Hard	Don't know
Obtaining a Sponsor or Champion who is clearly committed to supporting this project is . . .	1 Easy	2	3	4	5 Hard	Don't know
Achieving the customer's expectations will be . . .	1 Easy	2	3	4	5 Hard	Don't know
Defining the purpose and objectives for this project will be . . .	1 Easy	2	3	4	5 Hard	Don't know
The core processes for this project have been clearly documented.	Yes		No		Don't know	
The root cause of the problem/opportunity driving this project is well defined.	Yes		No		Don't know	
The assumptions associated with the project have been clearly identified.	Yes		No		Don't know	
The project benefits and validation measures have been clearly identified.	Yes		No		Don't know	
The project stakeholders have been clearly identified.	Yes		No		Don't know	
The project requires capital funds.	Yes		No		Don't know	
Alternative solutions have been identified for the project.	Yes		No		Don't know	

PMMG 1.2 TEAM CHARTER

Project ID:		Project Name:	

General Information

Project Requestor:		Project Request Date:	
Requestor s Manager:		Target Launch Date:	
Requestor s Department:		Project Manager:	

Project Description

Project Rationale

Initiative / Strategy Supported

Project Risk(s) If Not Implemented

Alternatives to Accomplish Project Objectives

Rough Order of Magnitude (Select most appropriate)

Level	Effort - Hrs	Est. Accuracy H-M-L	X

Resource Impact   discovery (initiation) effort only

Resource Name	Current Project(s) Impacted	ETC	Est. End Date

Steering Committee

Name	Representing

Action Taken	Date
Approved	
Denied	
Approved with modifications	
Additional information required	

Template concept compliments of Kelly Talsma, PMP

PMMG 1.3 POTENTIAL IMPACT

Project ID:		Project Name:	

Project Benefits

Benefit Description	Measurement to validate level of achievement

Project Deliverables

Deliverable Description	Review and approval requirements

Project Critical Success Factors (CSFs)

CSF Description	CSF Owner(s)

Project Cost-Benefit Analysis

Cost Factor	Amount
Estimated Project Budget	
Estimated Project Savings	
Return on Investment	
Net Present Value	

Project Integration

Department/Functions Impacted	Skills Required	Qty.

Project Risks

Risk Description	Impact (H-M-L)	Probability (H-M-L)

PMMG 1.4 PRELIMINARY COMMUNICATION PLAN

Project ID:		Project Name:	

Role	Who (names of people or groups)	What (what level of information is required)	When and How (frequency and method you use to communicate)
Project Customer			
Project Champion			
Project Sponsor			
Project Stakeholders			
Project Steering Team			
Project Team Members			
Suppliers/Vendors			
Management Team			
Others			

PMMG 1.5 SMALL PROJECT SUMMARY

Project ID:		Project Name:			Date:	
Assigned To:						

Project Purpose / Description:	Customer Expectations:

Deliverables:	Project Assumptions / Constraints:

In	Task Description	Status	Effort	Start	Finish
	Project Start:				
1	Requirements:				
2					
3					
4					
5	Analysis:				
6					
7					
8					
9	Design:				
10					
11					
12					
13	Build:				
14					
15					
16					
17	Test:				
18					
19					
20					
	Project Complete:				

PMMG 1.6 PROJECT SUMMARY

Project ID:	Project Name:			
Project Customer:	Functional Manager:	Sponsor:	Strategic Goal/Action Description:	Est. Budget: $

Project Purpose:	Project Description:
Requirements:	Expectations:

Project Objectives:	Deliverables:	Assumptions:	Milestones:	Duration (Day/Wk/Month):
			Est. Start	
			Initiation	
			Planning	
			Execution	
			Closing	
			Est. End	

Milestone Definitions:
Est. Start   Date when work will start on the project; make sure to allow time for review and approval of the Summary
Initiation   Time required to define the project requirements and analyze solutions
Planning   Time required to design the selected solution
Execution   Time required to develop and test the solution
Closing   Time required to implement the solution and obtain customer sign-off, archive project records
Est. End   Date when the project work will be completed

<Name> PROJECT BUDGET ESTIMATE

Cost Category		Mo1	Mo2	Mo3	Mo4	Mo5	Mo6	Mo7	Mo8	Mo9	Mo10	Mo11	Mo12	Total
Labor														
	<Type 1>													$ -
	<Type 2>													$ -
	<Type 3>													$ -
	Sub-Total	$ -	$ -	$ -	$ -	$ -	$ -	$ -	$ -	$ -	$ -	$ -	$ -	$ -
Equipment														
	<Type 1>													$ -
	<Type 2>													$ -
	<Type 3>													$ -
	Sub-Total	$ -	$ -	$ -	$ -	$ -	$ -	$ -	$ -	$ -	$ -	$ -	$ -	$ -
Hardware														
	<Type 1>													$ -
	<Type 2>													$ -
	<Type 3>													$ -
	Sub-Total	$ -	$ -	$ -	$ -	$ -	$ -	$ -	$ -	$ -	$ -	$ -	$ -	$ -
Software														
	<Type 1>													$ -
	<Type 2>													$ -
	<Type 3>													$ -
	Sub-Total	$ -	$ -	$ -	$ -	$ -	$ -	$ -	$ -	$ -	$ -	$ -	$ -	$ -
Suppliers														
	<Type 1>													$ -
	<Type 2>													$ -
	<Type 3>													$ -
	Sub-Total	$ -	$ -	$ -	$ -	$ -	$ -	$ -	$ -	$ -	$ -	$ -	$ -	$ -
	Travel													$ -
	Miscellaneous Costs													$ -
	TOTALS	$ -	$ -	$ -	$ -	$ -	$ -	$ -	$ -	$ -	$ -	$ -	$ -	$ -

197

PMMG 1.9 Scope Statement

Project Name:	Enter Project name

Project ID:	PMCoE will enter #	**Classification Level:**	PMCoE will enter #

CAR Number:	Enter CAR Number
Prepared By:	Enter name of person completing this Scope Statement
Date:	Enter date submitted for review
Customer:	Enter Customer Representative
Project Sponsor:	Enter Sponsor Representative
Project Manager:	Enter name of project manager

Project Stakeholders:	The people/organization/functional areas directly affected by the project. List the contact person representing each group.

Name:	**Representing:**	**Name:**	**Representing:**

Project Team Members:	The people directly involved in completing the work of the project or those assigned to represent them in planning and managing the project.

Name:	**Representing:**	**Name:**	**Representing:**

Project Steering Team	The people who will be assigned to the project Steering Team to act as project champions, cross-functional coordinators, and accountability overseers.

Name:	**Representing:**	**Name:**	**Representing:**

Associated Strategic Objective:	What strategic objective is this project aligned with? Enter MBP #, objective description, brief explanation of what aspect of the objective it will meet.

Project Purpose:	What is the primary purpose for the project? This is a summary statement of what the project will change.

Customer Expectations:	Be specific in listing what the customer expects to get from the project, i.e., lower cost, improved performance, higher quality, etc. •

Project Description:	This should be a definitive description. This information will help determine if future requests for changes to the project are within scope or outside of the original boundaries of the project deliverables. •

Business Benefits:	Benefits Measurements:
List the expected benefits the project will provide. Be specific, i.e., reduced cost by $xx, improve turn around time by xx days, reduce processing time by x%, etc. Benefits must be quantifiable and measurable. .	List the corresponding benefits metrics that will be used to validate that the benefits have been achieved. Also include the timing for obtaining the benefits. .

High Level Requirements:	List specific requirements, i.e., new hardware (specify), software (specify name and revision level), training, facilities, etc. .

Specific Inclusions:	List all the products, applications, systems, organizations, areas, etc., that are directly or indirectly affected by and/or are included in this project. Establish the boundaries (what is specifically included by design) of the project. .

Specific Exclusions:	List all the products, applications, systems, organizations, areas, etc., that are specifically excluded by this project. Establish what is outside the boundaries of the project (what is intentionally excluded by design). .

Project Deliverables:	List specific deliverables, i.e., hardware (specify), software (specify), training documents, processes and procedures, etc. This list should reflect what is noted in High Level Requirements as well as other specific things that are not. Deliverables must be tangible and recognizable as such. .

Project Constraints:	Identify specific limitations or predetermined targets (such as start/finish dates, budget limits, resource limits caused by limitation of availability or budget, outside constraints such as supplier delivery commitments, holidays, vacations, etc., that will impact project timing, cost, or quality. .

Project Assumptions:	These are known "unknowns." List assumptions that were used to establish initial timing, cost, and quality parameters for the project. Include the customer's assumptions as well. .

Project Success Factors:	List the factors that affect project success. Many of these also involve your assumptions, i.e., properly trained resources will be assigned to the project, unreasonable project milestone dates will not be established for the project, etc. .

Project Budget:
$

Project Milestone Plan	
Milestone Tasks	**Date**
Project Start	
Initiation Phase	
Planning Phase	
Execution Phase	
Closing Phase	
Project complete	

This Project Scope Statement has been reviewed and is approved, thereby authorizing the project team to proceed with further planning activities to meet the requirements of a Project Readiness Review prior to project start-up.

Readiness Review Date:	MM/DD/YY

The following individuals have reviewed and approved the project scope statement on the date entered.

Approved By		Date
Customer:		
Sponsor:		
Project Manager:		
PMCoE:	Dennis Bolles	

Project Scope Statement Change Log

This part of the document is used to record future changes to the project scope statement as they are approved.

Change Date	Changed By	Change Description

Note: All changes to this document __must__ be submitted and approved through the Project Change Control process before being incorporated into this document.

PMMG 1.10 PROJECT READINESS CHECKLIST

Project ID:		Project Name:				Level
Scheduled Review Date:						

Req d	PMMG Template	Are the following documents completed and /or processes in place?	Completed		Comments
			YES	NO	
	PMMG A	Project Status Update Cycle Established			
	PMMG B	Change Control Process Established			
	PMMG C	Issues Resolution Process Established			
	PMMG D	Steering Team Roles Defined			
	PMMG 1.7	Baseline Plan Completed and Approved			
	PMMG 1.8	Approved Project Budget			
	PMMG 1.9	Approved Scope Statement			
	PMMG 2.7	Team RRAA Matrix Completed			
	PMMG 2.8	Communication Plan Completed			
	PMMG 2.9	Risk Assessment Completed			
	PMMG 2.11	Metrics Plan Completed			
	PMMG 2.12	Configuration Management Plan Completed			
		CAR Approved			

Review sign-off required:

Project Champion:	Project Sponsor:	Project Manager:	PMCoE	Approved to Proceed:	
				Yes	No
Date:	Date:	Date:	Date:		

Comments:

PMMG 1.11

Project Portfolio Management Report

Report Period: (dd/mm to dd/mm)
Report Date: (dd/mm/yy)

Status Legend:
Green = On Schedule, Yellow = Late, Red = Over Due

Project ID	Project Name	Department	Project Manager	Start Date	End Date	Size (months)	Current Phase	Current Status	JA	FE	MR	AP	MY	JU	JL	AU	SE	OC	NO	DE
FY01-01	Example Project	IS Department	Joe Doe, PMP	15-Jan	15-Jun	6 months	Initiation													

FUTURE PROJECTS

Prelim. ID	Project Name	Department	Description

PMMG 2.1 PROCESS ANALYSIS

Project ID:		Project Name:	

Start

Stop

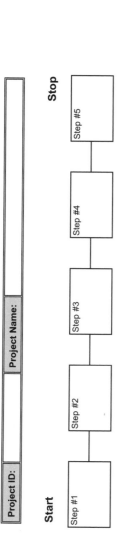

Step #1	Step #2	Step #3	Step #4	Step #5

Process Step Description

Step	Step Definition	Role(s)	Activity Definition

RRAA Matrix

Role	Responsibility	Accountability	Requisite Authority

PMMG 2.2 VOICE of the CUSTOMER / SPONSOR / PM

Project ID:		Project Name:	

Customer Name	Representing
What are the expectations?	
What are the assumptions?	
What are the constraints/limitations?	
What are the concerns?	

Sponsor Name	Representing
What are the expectations?	
What are the assumptions?	
What are the constraints/limitations?	
What are the concerns?	

Project Manager	Representing
What are the expectations?	
What are the assumptions?	
What are the constraints/limitations?	
What are the concerns?	

PMMG 2.3 CRITICAL TO QUALITY

Project ID:

Project Name:

Voice of the Customer	Issue / Driver	Specification (CTQ)

PMMG 2.4 Project Business Requirements

Project ID:	
Project Name:	
Customer:	
Sponsor:	
Manager:	
Corp. Goal:	

Project Description:	
Goals and Objectives:	
Customer Expectations:	
Customer Constraints:	

Requirement Category	Requirement Description
Hardware:	
Software:	
Consulting Services:	
Training:	
Specific Features:	
Project Timing:	
Constraints:	
Specific Skills:	
Other:	

Capital Funds Required?	Yes		No	

PMMG 2.5 Project Alternative Solutions

Date:	
Project ID:	
Project Name:	
Prepared By:	

Solution Criteria

Overview

Solution Criteria

Business Requirements (Goals and Objectives)

Ranking Criteria

Criteria Number	Brief Criteria Description	Requirement 1	Requirement 2	Requirement 3	Requirement 4	Total	Rank
1							
2							
3							
4							
5							
6							
7							

Degree of Variance	Description
3	Exceeds
2	Meets
1	Almost Meets
0	Does Not Meet

Alternative Solutions:

Alternative #1	
Alternative #2	
Alternative #3	

Alt.	Benefits	Problems
1	• • •	• • •
2	• • •	• • •
3	• • •	• • •
4	• • •	• • •
5	• • •	• • •

Evaluations of Alternatives

Alternative 1
Alternative 2
Alternative 3

Solution Criteria	Rank	Alt. 1	Alt. 2	Alt. 3	Alt. 4	Alt. 5
Total						

Degree of Variance	Description
3	Exceeds
2	Meets
1	Almost Meets
0	Does Not Meet

Recommendation:

PMMG 2.6 Project Records Administration

Project ID:	
Project Name:	

Filename	Description / Location	Author	Date	Rev
Initiation				
<Folder Name>				
<Folder Name>				
<Folder Name>				
<Folder Name>				

Project ID:
Project Name:

Work Element	PMMG Templates or Project File ID Number	Project Manager	Project Team Members	Project Customer	Project Sponsor	Project Steering Team	Project Supplier(s)	Project Administrator	PMCoE
PROJECT INITIATION									
Prepare Project Scope Statement	PMMG 1.9	R	I	A	A	I	I	S	A
Prepare Project Baseline Plan	PMMG 1.7	R	C	A	A	I	C	S	A
Perform Project Risk Assessment	PMMG 2.9	R	C	C	C	I	C	S	A
Prepare a Risk Management Plan		R	C	C	C	I	C	S	A
Prepare a Communication Plan	PMMG 2.8	R	C	C	C	I	C	S	A
Establish Project Records Administration (LAN Folders)	PMMG 2.6	A	C	C	I	I	C	R	I
Establish Issues Resolution Administration Procedures	Process C	A	C	C	I	I	C	R	I
Establish Change Control Administration Procedures	Process B	A	C	C	I	I	C	R	I
Establish Communications Administration		A	C	C	I	I	C	R	I
PROJECT PLANNING									
Establish Project Status Reporting Cycle	Process A	R	C	I	I	I	C	S	A
Establish (Review) Project Change Control Process		R	C	I	I	I	C	S	A
Establish (Review) Issue Resolution Process		R	C	I	I	I	C	S	A
Review Special Security Issues/Policies (if required)		R	I	A	A	I	I	S	I
Establish Scftware Configuration Management Processes		R	C	I	I	I	C	S	I
Establish Software Distribution Processes		R	S	I	I	I	S	S	I
Design User Training and Documentation Components		R	S	C	I	I	C	S	I
Develop Training Implementation Plan		R	S	S	S	I	S	S	I
PROJECT EXECUTION									
Perform Formal Checkpoint Reviews		R	S	S	S	A	C	S	S
Produce System Documentation		R	S	A	I	I	C	S	I
Produce User Training and Documentation		R	S	A	I	I	C	S	I
Develop System Test Plans, Cases, Data		R	S	C	I	I	C	S	I
Perform System Testing		R	S	I	I	I	C	S	I
Develop User Acceptance Test Plans, Cases, Data		R	S	I	I	I	C	S	I
Conduct Formal Acceptance Testing		R	S	A	I	I	C	S	I
Obtain Formal Approval For System Implementation		R	S	A	A	I	C	S	I
Conduct User Training		R	S	S	I	I	C	S	

PROJECT CLOSING									
Produce Help Desk Job Aids and Procedures		R	S	C				S	
Develop/Maintain User/Customer Request Process		R	S	S				S	S
Perform Post Project Survey	PMMG 4.1	C	C	C			C		
Hold Post Project Review	PMMG 4.2 +B15	S	S	I	I	S	I	S	R
Identify and Document Lessons Learned		S	S	I	I	S	I	S	R
Develop Process Improvement Strategies and Plans		C	C	C	I	C	C	C	R

LEGEND:
R - *Responsible* - Ensures that the work is done, may also contribute to the work
A - *Approves* - Signs off that the work was done (Concurs with the work)
S - *Support* - Supplies support and resources, does the work
    - If there is no 'S' for a row, the organization with the 'R' does the work
I - *Inform* - Informed of progress and of the results.
C - *Consults* - Supplies input and recommends solutions, consultation is mandatory

PMMG 2.8 Project Communication Plan

Project Name:
Project ID:

Communication Event	Facilitator	Purpose	Timing/Frequency	Participants	Location

PMMG 2.9 Project Risk Assessment

Probability and Impact Rating Values: High = 3, Medium = 2, Low = 1 (Probability x Impact = Severity Rating)

 Probability: High = 75–100% occurrence, Medium = 40–75% occurrence, Low = 0–40% occurrence

 Impact (cost/time/quality): High = > Major milestone impact; Medium-Noncritical path impact; Low = None or trivial impact

Priority Ratings: High = SR 6.0 – 9.0, Medium = SR 4.0 – 6.0, Low = SR 2.0 – 4.0

 High Priority Risks: require a detailed contingency plan and assigned responsibility
 Medium Priority Risks: require identified actions and are monitored regularly
 Low Priority Risks: only require identification and acknowledgment as acceptable project risks

Date:	
Project ID:	
Project Name:	

Risk #:						
Priority:		Probability:		Impact:		Severity Rating:
Task Line #:		Task Name:				
Risk Description:						
Internal/External:						
Actions:						
Contingency Plan:						

Risk #:						
Priority:		Probability:		Impact:		Severity Rating:
Task Line #:		Task Name:				
Risk Description:						
Internal/External:						
Actions:						
Contingency Plan:						

Risk #:						
Priority:		Probability:		Impact:		Severity Rating:
Task Line #:		Task Name:				
Risk Description:						
Internal/External:						
Actions:						
Contingency Plan:						

Project Risk Management Log

ID #	Description	Priority	Probability	Impact	IN or OUT	Owner	Estimated Occurrence Date

PMMG 2.10 Skills Inventory Matrix

Project ID:	Project Name:

Skill Codes

E = Expert
W = Working Knowledge
F = Familiar
N = No Experience Required
T= Training Needed

Roles/Team Members	Qty	Skill	Team Skills Inventory							

PMMG 2.11 Metrics Management Report

Project ID:	Project Name:
Date:	

Function	Element Measured	Granularity	Tool	Guidelines
Size				
Effort				
Staff				
Duration				
Resources				
Defects				
Change				
Environmental Characteristics				

Comments:

PMMG 2.12 CONFIGURATION MANAGEMENT

Project ID: [ ] Project Name: [ ]

Application/Document Name	Revision Level	Date Received / Revised	Date Testing Completed	Testing Completed By	Date Moved to Production / Released	Moved to Production / Released By

Meeting **AGENDA**	**\<Project Name\> Meeting**	
	Date: Time: Location: Contact Phone:	
Meeting Purpose: **Facilitator:**		
Participants:		
Time	**Agenda Topics**	**Presenter**

Special notes:

Key issues:

❖

MEETING OBJECTIVE:

❖

GROUND RULES:

❖ *All meetings will start on time*
❖ *Everyone will be on time*
❖ *One person speaks at a time*
❖ *All team members have an equal voice*
❖ *We respect each others' opinions*
❖ *We take our commitments seriously*
❖ *We hold each other accountable for commitments made*

PMMG 3.2 MEETING MINUTES
General Information

Project Name:	
Project ID Number:	
Meeting Purpose:	
Scribe:	
Facilitator:	
Date:	
Time:	
Location:	

Invitees/Attendees (Y= *in attendance,* N= *absent,* S= *substitute, G= Guest*)

Y,N,S,G	Name	Y,N,S,G	Name

Minutes

Agenda Topic	Main Points, Conclusions, Discussions, Decisions, Next Steps

Action Items

Item #	Open Date	Description	Assigned To	Target Date	Date Closed

Next Meeting Agenda Topics

Item #	Subject	Presenter
1.		
2.		
3.		

Next Meeting Date:	
Next Meeting Location:	

PMMG 3.3 Project Status Report

Project ID:		Project Name:	

Reporting Period:	Start Date:		End Date:	

Function/Area:		Function Leader:	

Scheduling Variances:

ID	Task Name	Planned Start	Actual Start	Planned Finish	Actual Finish	Total Variance
Countermeasure Plan:						
Countermeasure Plan:						
Countermeasure Plan:						
Countermeasure Plan:						

Critical Issues:

ID	Description	Enter Date	Assigned	Status

Pending Change Requests:

ID	Description	Enter Date	Function /Area	Status

PMMG 3.4 Issues Request Form

Project ID:		Project Name:	
Issues ID:		Category:	
Originator:			

Detailed Description

Impact to Plan (Budget/Schedule/Other)

Root Cause

Process Improvement to Prevent Future Occurrences

Associated change request number:	
Cost to implement this item:	
Hours to implement this item:	

Resolution/Decision

Resolution/Decision Date:	

PMMG 3.5 Issues Resolution Log

| Project ID: | |
| Project Name: | Last Updated: |

Status Code Legend
O = Open — Issue initially discovered.
R = Resolved — Issue has been resolved.
C = Canceled — The item is no longer an issue.

Priority Code Legend
L = Low, M = Medium, H = High

Issue ID #	Date Opened	Priority Code	Brief Description	Assigned to	Target Date	Closed Date

222

PMMG 3.6 Project Change Request Form

To Be Completed by Requestor

Task Name:		Request Type:		Problem		Change
Requested By:		Request Date:				
Organization:		Phone:				

Requester Priority:		Emergency		Urgent		Routine
Project/Group Leader:			Phone:			
Customer Support:			Phone:			
Description of Change:						
Benefit of/Reason for Change Request:						
Issues/Concerns with Change Request:						

Tracking Information   *To Be Completed by Project Team*

Change Request Report #:		Review Date:			
Proposed Solution:					
Impact of Change on System/Project:					
Change Request Report Review Comments:					
Disposition:		Approved		Rejected	Routine
Disposition Reason:					

Approvals *To Be Obtained by Project Manager*

Steering Team Chairperson	Date	Project Team Member	Date	Other	Date
Customer	Date	Sponsor	Date		

Assignment/Release Information- *To Be Completed by Project Manager*

Assigned To:		Date:	
Planned Release Date:			

PMMG 3.7 Project Change Control Log

Project ID: _____ Project Name: _____ Last Updated: _____

Change Request Report #	Description of Change	Assigned To	Planned Release Date	Release Version ID	Status	Status Date

Metrics Plan Tracking Report

Project ID:
Project Name:

Metric	Element Description	Plan	Mo1	Mo2	Mo3	Mo4	Mo5	Mo6	Mo7	Mo8	Mo9	Mo10	Mo11	Mo12	Totals
Size:	Scope Changes Approved														
Effort:															
Staff:															
Duration:	Schedule slippages														
Resources:															
Defects:															
Changes:															
Env. Char.:															
Other:															

PMMG 4.1 Post Project Review Survey

Project Name:	
Project ID:	
Name:	

Date Completed:	

Legend

0 = No Basis
1 = Strong No
2 = No
3 = Mixed Opinion
4 = Yes
5 = Strong Yes

Give a rating to each question according to the legend above.

1. Personal	0	1	2	3	4	5
Did you enjoy working on the project?						
Comment:						
Do you feel you have developed additional skills?						
Comment:						
Did you have the necessary skills to meet your objectives?						
Comment:						
Was the training on the project adequate?						
Comment:						
Did you find the work challenging/interesting?						
Comment:						

Legend

0 = No Basis
1 = Detrimental to the Project
2 = Little Value
3 = Some Use
4 = Very Useful
5 = Excellent

Give a rating to each standard according to the legend above.

2. Standards	0	1	2	3	4	5
Programming standards						
Documentation standards						
Testing standards						
Financial procedures						
Turnover procedures						
Status reports						
Project walk-thru's						
Team walk-thru's of subsystems						
Other (please specify)						

Do you feel the standards were adhered to?	Yes		No	

What additional standards should the project have developed?

```
0 = No Basis
1 = Strong No
2 = No
3 = Mixed Opinion
4 = Yes
5 = Strong Yes
```

Give a rating to each question according to the legend above.

3. Development Environment	0	1	2	3	4	5
Did you have the proper equipment needed for the project?						
Comment:						
Did you have adequate software to do your work?						
Comment:						
Were the tools and utilities useful? If not, why?						
Comment:						
Do you feel the recommended platform was a good choice?						
Comment:						
Was the overall business and technical design clear to you?						
Comment:						
Did you know where to find the design documentation?						
Comment:						
Was the level of documentation on the project adequate?						
Comment:						
Was the documentation handled in a well-structured manner?						
Comment:						
What procedures/methods would you use again?						
Comment:						
What procedures/methods would you NOT use again?						
Comment:						

Legend
0 = No Basis
1 = Failure
2 = Neither Failure or Success
3 = Limited Success
4 = Successful
5 = Very Successful

How well do you think the following was handled?

4. Testing	0	1	2	3	4	5
Unit Testing						
System Testing						
Turnovers						
Defect Reporting/Resolution						
Issues Reporting/Resolution						

Testing Comments:

_____

_____

_____

_____

_____

```
0 = No Basis
1 = Failure
2 = Neither Failure or Success
3 = Limited Success
4 = Successful
5 = Very Successful
```

How successful/useful were the project communications?

5. Communications	0	1	2	3	4	5
Between colleagues?						
Between you and your direct supervisor?						
Between you and the project manager?						
Between you and the customer?						
On overall project status?						
On the objectives of the project?						
On your objectives?						
On your performance?						
On the objectives of the development team?						
On project decisions?						
On project issues?						
On team issues?						

Communication Comments:

_____

_____

_____

Legend

0 = No Basis
1 = Failure
2 = Neither Failure or Success
3 = Limited Success
4 = Successful
5 = Very Successful

How well do you think the following was handled?

6. Planning/Scheduling/Status Reporting	0	1	2	3	4	5
How would you rate the overall project planning?						
Comment:						
How would you rate the overall project scheduling?						
Comment:						
Was it difficult to meet deadlines?						
Comment:						
Did you feel involved enough in planning/scheduling?						
Comment:						
Did you feel involved enough in estimation of your work?						
Comment:						
Did you feel comfortable raising issues?						
Comment:						
Were issues you raised dealt with adequately?						
Comment:						
Did you feel the hours you worked were too long?						
Comment:						
If you worked long hours, did you feel pressured into it?						
Comment:						

7. Methodologies

In your opinion, what methodologies did the project use?

_____

_____

_____

How well did they work?

_____

_____

_____

Why?

_____

_____

_____

Additional Comments:

_____

_____

_____

8. Summary Points

What in your opinion were the three main project strengths?

_____

_____

_____

What in your opinion were the three main project weaknesses?

_____

_____

_____

In your opinion, was enough attention paid to quality in both the development process and the final product?

_____

_____

Any other comments you would like to add?

_____

PMMG 4.2 Post Project Review Report

Project ID:			
Project Name:			
Project Description:			
Total Duration:			
Start Date:		End Date:	
Forecasted Hours:		Actual Hours:	
Budgeted Dollars:		Actual Dollars:	
Forecasted Resources:		Actual Resources:	

Significant Impacts to the Project

Issue 1

Description
Impact
Suggestions for Improvement

Issue 2

Description
Impact
Suggestions for Improvement

Lessons Learned
Project Initiation and Controlling

Project Lesson	Knowledge Learned

Project Planning and Controlling

Project Lesson	Knowledge Learned

Project Execution and Controlling

Project Lesson	Knowledge Learned

Project Closing and Controlling

Project Lesson	Knowledge Learned

PMMG 4.3 Metrics Report

Project ID:	Project Name:
Date:	

Function	Granularity	Tool	Guidelines	Measurements		
				High	Low	Average
Size:						
Effort:						
Staff:						
Duration:						
Resources:						
Defects:						
Change:						
Environmental Characteristics:						

Comments:

INDEX

A

Achieving corporate goals and objectives, 36-38
Alternative solutions template, 207-208
Assembling project and steering teams, 24
Assessment methods requirements, 159-162
Authorization, 115-118
  activities during process, 115
  charter, 116
  definition, 30
  overview, 115
  process flowchart, 116
  process for project portfolio, 51, 52, 54, 55
  request, 115-116
  RRAA matrix, 118
  steps for, 117
  task force team scope, 29
  templates/tools, 116

B

Baseline schedule, 66, 67, 68
Baumgardner, Dwane, 36-38
Benchmarking, 96, 97-99
  challenges to overcome, 98-99
  importance of, 98-99
  project management knowledge network, 96
  trust development, 99
Budget estimate template, 197
Business requirements template, 206

C

Capacity and capability, 43-47
  determining, 43-47
project estimating standards, 43, 44-46
project portfolio management system, 43, 46-47
standard time recording, 43
workers' skills and knowledge, 43-44
Capital authorization request, 61, 107, 119, 120, 139
Capital budget plan, 47-48, 49-50. *See also* Strategic planning process
CAR. *See* Capital authorization request
Certification program, 77-78
Changes
  control log template, 224
  control process, 131, 134-137
  control process flowchart, 134
  control process steps, 135
  request form template, 223
  RRAA matrix, 136
  steps leading to, 6
  templates/tools, 134
Charter
  elements of, 21-22
  information included in, 21-22
  project, 116
  purpose of, 21
  sample, 170-172
  team template, 192
  writing, 21-22
Classifications, creating, 61-62
Closing, project, 105, 106, 139-145
  activities during, 139
  metrics reporting process, 140, 143-145
  overview, 139

Closing, project *(continued)*
    post project review process,
        139-140, 141-142
    RRAA matrix, 142, 145
    steps, 141, 144
    templates/tools, 140
Communication plan, 66, 67
    preliminary plan template, 194
    sample template, 212
    template, 212
Configuration management
        template, 217
Core process template, 108-109
Corporate Project/Program
        Management Office (CPMO), ix,
        7, 8, 9
Creating and managing project
        portfolio. *See* Project portfolio,
        creating and managing

D
Deming, 37, 38-39, 40
Driving focus, 4-7

E
Education and training, 73-80,
        147-167
    assessment methods requirements,
        159-162
    benefits, 77
    certification program, 77-78
    curriculum, 73, 150, 163-167
    curriculum requirements,
        163-167
    definition, 32
    delivery consortium, 79
    developing program for, 78-79
    elements of, 74-76
    goals, 75-76, 147, 148-149
    goals matrix, 148
    importance of, 74
    knowledge objectives
        requirements, 151-154
    learning objectives requirements,
        155-158
    overview, 147
    participant groups, 147, 150

    requirements, 74-76, 147, 150,
        151-162
    success factors, critical, 73-80
    summary, 79-80
    task force team, 31
Elements of PMCoE, four key,
        29-32
Establishing, 1-99
    creating and managing project
        portfolio, 35-56
    education and training, 73-80
    initiating, 19-33
    introduction, 3-18
    key ingredients of methodology,
        57-71
    maturity, 87-99
    motivation for, 5-6
    readiness, 81-85
Evaluation survey, project, 176-177
Execution, project, 105, 106,
        127-137
    activities during, 127
    change control process, 131,
        134-137
    issues resolution process, 128, 131,
        132-133
    metrics tracking, 131, 137
    overview, 127
    progress reporting cycle process,
        127-128, 129-130
    reporting cycle process flowchart,
        128
    reporting process, 130
    reporting process steps, 129
    templates/tools, 128

G
Goals, 3, 57
Goals and objectives
    achieving corporate, 36-38
    identifying organizational, 35-36

H
Hoshin kanri, 37, 38-42
    benefit of, 38
    definition, 38, 40
    translations for, 40

I

Identifying organizational goals and objections, 35-36
Impact potential template, 193
Implementation group positioning, 3
Information technology as starting point, 6-7
Ingredients of methodology, key, 57-71. *See also* Methodology
Initiation phase, 19-33, 105, 106, 119-122
    activities during, 119
    assembling project and steering teams, 24
    assess knowledge and skill levels, 19-21
    authorization, 30, 32
    charter writing, 21-22
    education, 32
    elements, four key, 29, 30, 32
    kick-off event, 25-28
    overview, 119
    process, 119-122
    process flowchart, 120
    readiness, 32
    RRAA matrixes, 112
    scope statement writing, 22-24
    standards, 30, 32
    steps, 121
    summary, 32-33
    task force teams creation, 28-29, 30, 31
    templates/tools, 120
Introduction, 3-18
    driving forces, 4-7
    importance of positioning, 10-11
    naming, 7-10
    organization roles, 14, 15-17
    organization structure, 12-14
    organization titles, 8
    project management as business function, 11-12
    reporting scenarios, 13-14
    reporting structure, 10
    summary, 14, 17-18
    viewed as business function, 11-12

Issues
    request form template, 221
    resolution log template, 222
    resolution process, 128, 131, 132-133
    resolution process steps, 132
    RRAA matrix, 133
IT. *See* Information technology

J

Juran, Joseph M., 39

K

Kerzner, Dr. Harold, 4-5
Kick-off event, 25-28
    agenda, 25, 27-28
    planning phase and, 123
    planning steps, 27
    proposal for, 26
    publicizing ways, 25
    purpose, 26
Knowledge and skill levels assessment, 19-21
Knowledge objectives requirements, 151-154

L

Learning objectives requirements, 155-158
Levels, project, 106-113
Logo, 55-56

M

Management by objectives (MBO), 39
Management by planning (MBP), 36-38, 40-42, 47
Management of environment flowchart, 91
Management of organizational change flowchart, 92
Management of products flowchart, 90
Management of projects flowchart, 89
Management team survey, 19-20, 173-175

Managing organizations by projects
(MOBP), 88, 89-90
Maturity, 87-99
  benchmarking, 96, 97-99
  characteristics, 97
  definition, 87
  model diagram, 95
  models, 87-88
  organization maturing diagram, 94
  project management maturity
    survey, 178-188
  stages of, 93-96, 97
  summary, 99
Maturity level. *See* Knowledge and
    skills levels assessment
Meeting agenda template, 218
Meeting minutes template, 219
Methodology. *See also* Methodology
    guidelines; Methodology
    introduction
  classifications creation, 61-62
  contents list, 60
  criticism of, common, 65
  definition, 58
  distributing project management
    methodology, 69-70
  generic, 59-61
  guidelines, 101-167
  ingredients, key, 57-71
  introduction, 103-113
  requirements for early
    implementers, minimum, 62-68
  resistance, overcoming, 63-64
Methodology guidelines, 101-167
  authorization, 115-118
  closing, project, 105, 106, 139-145
  contents list, 60
  controlling processes, 106
  diagram of, 59
  education and training, 147-167
  execution, 105, 106, 127-137
  ingredients, 60
  initiation, 105, 106, 119-122
  introduction, 103-113
  map, 105
  phases, 106
  planning, 105, 106, 123-126

templates, 68
tools, 66, 68
Methodology introduction, 103-113
  controlling processes, 108
  core process integration, 105-106,
    108-109
  elements diagram, 105
  implementation, 104
  levels, project, 106-113
  map, 105
  overview, 104-105
  phase definitions, 106
  purpose, 103-104
  vision, 103
Metrics
  management report template, 216
  plan tracking report template, 225
  report template, 234
  reporting process, 140, 143-145
  tracking, 131
  tracking templates/tools, 137, 143

N
Naming the function, 7-10

O
Objectives and goals
  achieving corporate, 36-38
  identifying organizational, 35-36
Organization
  roles, 14, 15-17
  structure, 8, 9-10, 12-14
  titles and responsibilities, 8,9
Organization Project Management
    Maturity Model (OPM3), 87, 95
Organizational goals and objectives,
    identifying, 35-36

P
PeopleSoft, 44
Planning phase, 105, 106, 123-126
  elements, 123
  overview, 123
  process, 123-126
  process flowchart, 124
  RRAA matrix, 126
  steps, 125

strategic forecast planning
   template, 190
template/tools, 124
PMCoE. *See* Project Management
   Center of Excellence
Positioning importance, 10-11
Post project review
   process, 139-140, 141-142
   report template, 233
   survey template, 226-232
Process analysis template, 203
Process step description, 111-112
Project and steering teams,
   assembling, 24
Project classification matrix, 107
Project estimating standards, 43,
   44-46
   criteria for claiming progress, 46
   methodology, 45-46
   metrics used, 44, 45
   recognizing time performance,
   46
Project Evaluation Survey, 20,
   176-177
Project management
   as business function, 11-12
   methodology distribution, 69-70
   resistance, overcoming, 63-64
Project Management Body of
   Knowledge (PMBOK) Guide, 58,
   59, 61, 73, 77, 103, 104
Project Management Center of
   Excellence
   driving forces, 4-7
   elements, four key, 29, 30, 32
   focus of, ix
   goal, main, 57
   goals, 3
   implementation group, 3-4
   initiating, 19-33
   logo for, 56
   motivations for establishing, 5-6
   names for, other, ix, 7
   organization roles, 14, 15-17
   responsibility definition, 8
   structure of, 8, 9-10
   support for, 3

Project Management Institute (PMI),
   77, 87, 95, 103, 104
Project management knowledge
   network, 96
Project Management Maturity
   Survey, 20, 178-188
Project management methodology
   guideline (PMMG), 103-105. *See
   also* Methodology guidelines
   templates, 189-234
Project management office (PMO),
   ix, 7, 8, 9, 10
Project Management Professional
   (PMP), 77, 80
Project managers report scenarios,
   13-14
Project office (PO), ix, 7, 8, 9, 10
Project portfolio, creating and
   managing, 35-56
   access to information needed, 53
   authorization process, 51, 52, 54,
   55
   benefits, 47
   capacity and capability, 43-47
   capital budget plan and, 47-48,
   49-50
   establishing, 43
   goals and objectives, achieving
   corporate, 36-38
   goals and objectives, identifying
   organizational, 35-36
   Hosin kanri, 38-42
   information needed, 51
   logo, 55-56
   management report template, 202
   managing, 48, 51, 53-55
   opportunities, new, 48, 51, 52
   reviews, 53, 55
   steps description, 49
   summary, 56
Project portfolio management
   system, 46-47
Project profile: strategic forecast
   planning template, 190
Project review process
   description, 83
   flowchart, 82

Project selection template, 191
Project summary template, 196
Project support office (PSO), ix, 7, 8, 9,
    10
Publicizing creation of PMCoE, 25

Q
Quality template, critical to, 205

R
Readiness, 81-85
    checklist, 84
    checklist template, 201
    definition, 32
    planning phase and, 123
    post project reviews, 84-85
    review, 82-84
    summary, 85
    task force team, 31
Records administration template,
    209-211
Reporting scenarios, 13-14
Reporting structure, 8, 9-10
Request, project, 115-116, 117-118
Risk assessment, 66, 67
    template, 213-214
Risk management log sample form,
    project, 214
RRAA matrix
    authorization process, 54, 118
    change control process, 136
    initiation process, 122
    issues resolution process, 133
    planning process, 126
    post project review process, 142, 145
    process flow diagram, 113
    progress reporting process, 130
    strategic forecast plan, 50

S
Scope of work (SOW). *See* Scope
    statement
Scope statement
    adjusting, 61
    definition, 66-67
    elements of, 23

importance of, 66
modifying, 107
project initiation and, 119
project planning and, 123
for task force teams, 29, 30, 31
template, 198-200
writing, 22-24
Skill level and knowledge assessment,
    19-21
Skills inventory matrix template, 215
Small project summary template, 195
Solutions template, project alternative,
    207-208
Standard time recording, 43
Standards
    definition, 30, 57
    task force team, 30
Statistical quality control (SQC), 39
Status report template, project, 220
Steering and project teams,
    assembling, 24
Steps leading to change, 6
Strategic forecast planning template,
    190
Strategic planning process (SPP)
    management by planning (MBP)
        and, 47
    process design, 48
    RRAA matrix, 50
    step description, 49
Survey participation, 20-21

T
Task force teams creation, 28-29, 30,
    31
Team charter template, 192
Tools, 169-188
Training and education. *See* Education
    and training

V
Voice of the customer/sponsor/PM
    template, 204

W
Worker's skills and knowledge, 43-44